DINA
ASHER-
SMITH

ULTIMATE SPORTS HEROES

DINA ASHER-SMITH

GOING FOR GOLD

DINO

First published by Dino Books in 2021,
an imprint of Bonnier Books UK,
The Plaza, 535 King's Road, London SW10 0SZ
Owned by Bonnier Books,
Sveavägen 56, Stockholm, Sweden

🐦 @dinobooks
www.bonnierbooks.co.uk

Paperback ISBN: 9781789463040
E-book ISBN: 9781789464368

British Library cataloguing-in-publication data:
A catalogue record for this book is available from the British Library.

Printed and bound in Great Britain by Clays Lltd, Elcograf S.p.A.

1 3 5 7 9 10 8 6 4 2

TABLE OF CONTENTS

TABLE OF CONTENTS

CHAPTER 1

STRAIGHT INTO THE DUCK POND

Winston Asher-Smith breathed a deep sigh of satisfaction as he walked through the chalk meadows and woodlands of High Elms Country Park in Orpington. He stopped and turned to his wife, Julie, and the two of them took in the beautiful view towards the North Downs that stretched before them.

'It's such a relief we have this on our doorstep. It makes the commute into London each day just about bearable, knowing we can come here at the weekends.'

Winston worked as a mechanical engineer in the

city, and like most other commuters, he struggled with the daily grind.

'When you're squeezed into a tube train with someone's armpit in your face, I try and imagine I'm walking through the fields here.'

Julie looked at him and laughed. 'That can't be easy to imagine!' She looked off into the distance thoughtfully. 'Sometimes when the wind rushes through the branches here, I pretend it's the sound of the sea. And just for a second I fool myself that I can smell the coffee growing, wafting down from the Blue Mountains.'

He looked at her and smiled. 'Yes, the sea, I miss it too.'

Winston and Julie were both originally from Jamaica but had made the UK their home.

'There is Kingston in Shoreham of course, down on the south coast. That's only 20 minutes away,' said Julie.

They both laughed.

'Not sure I'd get in the sea there any time of year

– even during a heatwave! Brrr!' said Winston.

'Yeah, we don't have many of those here, but at least we don't have to worry about hurricane season.'

'Good point,' Winston sighed. 'But I do miss my sprint days, running along the beach.'

'Mama!'

They stopped to both look down at their two-year-old daughter, Dina, who was starting to get agitated and restless in her pushchair. She was looking up at them impatiently, her big brown eyes imploring them to take her out.

'What is it, apple pie?' her father asked. Dina's grandmother had coined this nickname because she thought her grandchild had the sweetest smile she'd ever seen, with the sweetest nature to match. The name had stuck. But, from the moment Dina had learnt to crawl, she had been an active child and her sunny nature could change if she was put in a pushchair or buggy for too long.

'We'd better take her out now,' said Julie. 'She

won't sleep otherwise.'

She bent down to undo the straps on Dina's chair and said: 'You don't like being cooped up for too long, do you?'

Dina beamed as she began to wriggle free, and Julie added: 'You never seem to get tired on those legs of yours either!'

'Hardly a surprise is it? What with my athletic prowess,' Winston chuckled.

'Er, excuse me, I was a demon on that hockey pitch back in the day. I used to run rings round the other team. In fact, when Dina's a little older, I'll start teaching her.'

'Yeah, but it's not real running, is it, just a bit of skipping about.'

'What?! I'm an excellent runner! I did a great time in the 800-metre race with the Herne Hill Harriers.'

'Amateurs!'

'At least I still run. You're so out of practice I bet I'd hardly have to lift a finger against you in a sprint now.'

'We'll see about that. Race you to that tree!' Winston pointed in the direction of a giant oak just over a hundred metres away.

'Easy!' Julie laughed and went to bend down as if at a starting block. She then turned round in a panic.

'Dina? Dina?!'

While they teased each other, Dina had taken the chance to climb out of her buggy and make a bolt for freedom.

'There she is!'

Winston pointed towards Dina, who was heading off in the distance towards a duck pond at the foot of the hills. She was toddling at great speed and had already covered a lot of ground. They both sped after her, no longer concerned with who got there first.

Dina stopped for a second and looked back at them, laughing, her eyes shining.

'Quack, quack!' She pointed at the ducks, her

short, dark curls bouncing, and sped on towards the edge of the pond.

Her parents shouted after her. A couple of onlookers watched in shock as she accelerated. One rushed forward in an attempt to reach her but couldn't catch her before her legs reached the water. She showed no sign of slowing down as she went splashing into the shallow depths of the pond, still laughing at the startled ducks, who noisily flew away in a cloud of feathers.

Winston waded into the pond and lifted Dina out. He reassured Julie, who was just behind him: 'Don't worry, it's not too deep.'

'Dina, are you alright?! Who knows what's in that pond!'

'She seems okay, just rather wet!'

As Dina took in the angry and serious faces of her breathless parents, her joyful expression crumpled.

'Oh Dina – it's alright!' They both comforted her as she burst into tears. 'But don't ever do that again!'

She turned back to look at the ducks. 'Splash, splash!'

'I've never seen a little kid run so fast!' They both turned around to see the shocked face of one of the passers-by.

'Neither have we!' said Dina's parents in unison.

'You've got your work cut out for you, running around after that one.'

'She couldn't wait to get in the water!'

Julie and Winston turned to face each other.

'I think we might have to think about swimming lessons.'

'Or sort out some sort of alarm system if she runs over a metre! We can't let her out of our sight for a second!'

CHAPTER 2

SPORTS
DAY

Dina took a deep breath and began to blow into her trumpet, determined to nail the tricky intro to the *William Tell* Overture. She sighed in frustration as she fumbled over the first few notes for the third time. Her teacher looked at her in surprise.

'Everything alright, Dina?'

'Yep. Sorry, I'll try again.' Dina always stuck at things if she didn't get them right the first time. From firing golf balls into the flowerpots at the back of the garden with her dad to scoring against her mum when they played hockey together on the street, she always told herself: 'I'll try harder next time, until I get it right.'

She normally loved playing the trumpet, but she couldn't focus that morning. She kept gazing out of the window of her school's music block. It was a beautiful sunny day with a gentle breeze blowing. Just perfect for Perry Hall Primary School's sports day. She was almost too excited at the prospect of running that afternoon for her sports team in the relay race. It was her first year at primary school and Miss Papadopoulos had asked her to run the last leg, or anchor, of the race for their house team, which was a mix of students from different year groups in the school: 'You're the anchor, Dina!'

Dina knew her teacher had noticed how fast she ran and that she'd been chosen to make the difference on those vital last metres of the home stretch. She also knew her mum would be watching that afternoon and she wanted to make her proud too. She felt a mixture of fear and excitement and vowed to run the best that she could for the team. 'I want us to win,' she said to herself over and over.

'I want to win.'

She barely managed to contain her excitement for the rest of the lesson. She normally wolfed down her chicken drumsticks at lunch, but on this occasion she could only pick at them. As she was changing into her PE kit, her friends chattered and laughed around her in the school's changing rooms, while she felt her nerves rising. Wow, why weren't they more nervous? They didn't seem that bothered about winning.

Her friend Nicole put her arm around her. 'Dina, don't worry, you'll smash it for us.'

Dina smiled back and laughed but could feel the adrenaline rising inside her.

'It's just a race,' Nicole added.

Dina laughed and shrugged. 'Sure, I know.'

But deep down she knew it meant something to her. It always meant something to her. Whether she was swimming, playing hockey, dancing or playing the trumpet, she wanted to win and enjoyed it when she did. She walked out to the field thinking of her idol, Serena Williams, and tried to imagine how she must feel walking out on to the court each time. Her heart beat a little faster as she remembered something that she'd heard Serena say in an interview. 'Tennis is mostly mental. You win or lose the match before you even go out there.' Dina imagined how good she would feel crossing the line first and smiled to herself. She instantly felt a little calmer.

Dina cheered on her teammates who blitzed their way through the egg-and-spoon race, bean bag throwing competition and the hula hoop challenge. Miss Papadopoulos jumped up and down with excitement too as they picked up top points throughout. But then they faced tough competition from some seasoned sprinters in the upper school and fell behind by several points. It was time for the 4 x 100 metres relay race, the last race. Miss Papadopoulos gathered Dina and her three other teammates together.

'Okay guys, who wants to win the cup for

our house?!'

'Me!' They all shouted in unison.

'Okay! So just remember: don't look behind for the baton, just wait until you feel it in your hands, look straight ahead and run! You can do this!'

Dina took her place on the track. She knew how tricky baton changes were from watching them on the TV; it was a hard technique to perfect in athletics because of the speed of the runners. The crowd cheered as the first leg took off and Dina beamed as she heard her mum rooting for each runner on her team.

The first runner hadn't made a great start and was trailing behind in fourth place by the time the second runner took the baton. Dina watched the second runner's ponytail swish from side to side as she made up some ground to take third before passing to the third runner.

While Dina cheered, she thought to herself, *not long now*. She had her work cut out for her, as two of the runners had already changed over, but she knew she was a fast sprinter and that she could make a difference in this last leg.

She waited with bated breath while the runner on the third leg ran down the field towards her, the baton glinting in the afternoon sun. She held out her left palm as straight as possible for the handover. The second she felt the baton in her hand she gripped it as tightly as possible before sprinting down the field.

'Go Dina!' she heard her team cheer. She made up a lot of ground on the two who'd taken the lead, their T-shirts flailing behind them in the wind.

'I can catch them,' she said to herself. At 10 metres, then 20 metres, she was hot on their heels. She felt amazing, as though her body was gliding through the air. She broke out into a smile as she overtook each runner, one by one, until she effortlessly crossed the finish line. She threw her hands behind, like the serious athletes she'd seen on the TV. Then she caught sight of her mum jumping up and down for joy among the crowd of mums that had gathered at the front, their jaws agape in astonishment. Then she heard Miss Papadopoulos's voice: 'Dina, that was incredible! You flew like the wind!'

She felt her teammates' arms around her, lifting her up and cheering: 'Dina! Dina!' They'd done it. She'd done it. As her team lifted the winning trophy, she knew she'd been important in their win. And this was a feeling she wanted more of.

CHAPTER 3

RUNNING CLUB

'Race you to the swings!'

'What's the point Dina, you're too fast!'

But it was too late. Dina had already shot off ahead of her friend Nicole down the path through Poverest Park, her two plaits flying behind her in the wind. Located just behind Dina's house and next to her school, it provided a wide-open space for them to play in.

Nicole caught up with Dina, who was already sitting on the swing, her brown eyes twinkling as she leisurely swung her feet, smiling joyfully. Nicole knew there was no smugness or spite in her expression; Dina just loved running, simple as that.

'You're not even out of breath!' gasped Nicole.

'It's all the swimming I do. My teacher says it keeps my lungs strong.'

Dina was never one to brag about her talent, and Nicole smiled. She had a suggestion to make: 'You should join the school's running club.'

Dina shrugged. 'I dunno.'

It was a few days after sports day and her friends were still talking about Dina's run. But she wasn't sure if she wanted to join another club. From dancing to diving and Brownies, she loved to take part in many different sports and activities.

'Come with me this Monday lunchtime,' said Nicole.

'Maybe.'

'Oh, go on! I'll buy you an ice cream if you do!'

A smile spread over Dina's face. Nicole knew how to persuade her. Frozen treats of any flavour were a staple favourite.

'What, now?'

Nicole sighed and felt around for loose change in her pocket. 'If it gets you to running club.'

'Race you to the ice cream van then!'

***

Dina spent the morning gazing out of the window at the school's field track. Her class were learning about the Ancient Greeks. She found this period of history fascinating; in particular she loved to read the myths and learn about the strength and power that the gods and goddesses possessed. When she got home from school she excitedly recounted some of her favourite stories to her parents: Theseus slaying the Minotaur, Icarus flying too close to the sun or Athena beating Poseidon to become the patron goddess of Athens.

She sighed and thought to herself: 'I reckon it would be alright to be a god or goddess. They definitely had lots of fun and could do all sorts of things with their strength and power.' She thought about the modern-day heroes she admired: Serena Williams, Kelly Holmes. They might not be able to make fire, whip up storms or fight monsters, but they were the closest equivalent that she could think of.

Learning about the Ancient Greeks wasn't the only reason she loved Mondays though. As the clock ticked towards lunchtime, she grew more and more excited. She couldn't wait to get out on to the track for running club.

In her first week at the club her teacher, Mrs Carty, was taken aback by Dina's speed. After a quick warm-up, she gave some pointers on the best way to run: 'Keep your upper body as relaxed as possible and don't expel all your energy to begin with.'

Then, Mrs Carty encouraged the children to run along beside her as they took on the first lap of the field.

'Okay, now go at your own pace, gently does it to start. Don't put pressure on yourself to keep up with me.'

She started off at a steady pace with 10 girls following behind her before she increased her speed. Before long, she heard the sound of someone's feet pounding behind her. She turned to look just as Dina drew up beside her, a broad smile slowly spreading across her face.

'Hi, Miss!' she said.

'Hi Dina! Are you enjoying your first day at running club?' She asked the question with a knowing smile. The answer was already clear.

As the weeks progressed, Dina started to overtake her teacher with seemingly little effort, and Mrs Carty found herself struggling to keep up with her.

'Hi again, Miss!' she quipped as she ran past her for the second and third time round the lap.

On one occasion, she admitted to Dina: 'I never thought I'd struggle to keep up with a seven-year-old child but you really are fast!' Although she was cautious not to praise Dina too much, she also noticed the girl's humility; during running club,

Dina was kind to the other children and gave them advice on how to warm up their muscles.

The teachers could see that Dina was in her element when she ran around the field and loved the opportunity to shine. Dina was enjoying running more and more, although she still enjoyed all her other hobbies. However, that summer her parents encouraged her to try out other track and field events. On the first day of the holidays, Dina headed for Perry Hall's athletics club. Her eyes lit up as she saw the size of the field track with its proper white lane markings, just like the ones she saw in the stadiums on TV, as well as the sand-filled runway and horizontal bar for long jump and high jump. In the distance, she saw children practising their javelin and discus throws.

One afternoon their teacher, Mr Hewitt, set out six hurdles for the children to practise as a warm-up. Dina smiled as she saw the obstacles stretching out before her. She couldn't wait to leap over them.

Mr Hewitt instructed them: 'Stay tall, keep your

body forward and don't lean back. Bend and lift with your knee.' Dina could barely take his words in as she sized up the height of them and got in her lane alongside the other children.

'On your marks, get set – go!'

Dina tore off down the track towards the first hurdle, and bounced over it lightly, lifting her right knee instinctively. She cleared the next three gleefully before running towards the finishing line. She looked back to see the other children behind her, either knocking the hurdles over or plodding cautiously over each one. Mr Hewitt shook his head in amazement.

At the end of the day, Dina bounded over to her mother with a huge smile on her face. 'That was so much fun!'

'What did you enjoy the most?'

'All of it! But I really loved the hurdles.'

Mr Hewitt walked over to speak to them both.

'She flew over them like a gazelle!' he said, shaking his head in disbelief. 'You don't have springs in your feet do you, Dina?'

Dina's mother laughed.

'No, they're just ordinary trainers, I promise,' said Dina.

'Well, if you approach all your events as you approached those hurdles, you've got a bright future ahead of you as an athlete.'

Dina smiled at these words. She thought of all the athletes she watched on TV. For now, running was just for fun. But could she be just like one of them, one day? Her heart soared at the thought of it.

CHAPTER 4

THE
BEES

It was a cold and wet November morning and there was a mist descending around the lake in Crystal Palace Park. As Dina trampled through the mud and soggy wet leaves on the ground, she began to regret agreeing to take part in the Bromley Primary Schools Cross Country Championships. This was the third time her PE teacher, Miss Hudson, had picked her, and she knew it was because she was good. Up against 54 other primary schools, Dina helped her school team finish near the top five and had consistently finished in some of the highest places across the county.

She shivered as she felt the damp seep through her waterproof running jacket and thought gratefully of the hot chocolate and treats she knew would be awaiting her at the finishing line. Crowds had lined the route to cheer on the runners. Dina vowed this would be the last time she ran long distance. No amount of coaxing from Miss Hudson would persuade her again.

She groaned to herself as she continued to trudge through the mud. 'When will this end?'

But it wasn't long before the cheers from the crowd grew even louder and she realised she was approaching the last hundred metres. 'Not long till my hot chocolate!' This comforting thought spurred her on past the finishing line. As she crossed it, she saw Mrs Carty and Miss Hudson cheering and waving at her, huddled together under an umbrella. Then she saw her mum, who looked even more excited than usual. Her dad was just behind her, chatting away to people in the crowds but, as always, keeping a look out for Dina.

Her mum rushed forward to hug her, swiftly followed by her dad. 'You've won!'

'What?' Dina was gobsmacked.

Her mum handed her a cup of hot chocolate and threw a big fleece-lined sou'wester around her. 'Well done, Dina! I think you've finished even faster than last time – just under 20 minutes!'

Miss Hudson and Mrs Carty came over to congratulate her too.

'One of the fastest times in the whole county, I bet!' said Miss Hudson.

Dina was very happy to win, but then she remembered the promise she'd made to herself. She stared at the four of them defiantly, as the rain continued to beat down.

'I've had enough of this. I'm not doing it again.'

'Ah Dina, once you've warmed up you'll change your mind,' said Miss Hudson.

'No, I love running. But I don't want to do long distance. I just want to sprint from now on.'

She'd never said it out loud before but suddenly

it completely made sense to her.

The four of them looked at her and then nodded their heads in agreement.

'When you sprint, you always have a smile on your face,' said her mother. 'I'd rather you did that if it makes you happy.'

'Yeah,' said her dad, 'you do look a bit grumpy at the moment!'

'You would if you'd just been running through 1800 metres of mud and sludge!' said her mum.

'Congratulations, Dina!'

Dina heard a friendly voice behind her. She turned around and looked up to see an equally friendly face of a man she'd never seen before.

'Not a nice day to be running, eh. Have you warmed up yet?'

Dina's hands were gripping her hot chocolate. 'Just about.' She smiled.

He held his hand out to Dina's parents. 'Hi, I'm John. I'm from Blackheath and Bromley Harriers. Have you heard of us?'

They all nodded. Dina most certainly had. The athletics club was one of the oldest in south-east London and was known for producing a fair number of sporting legends.

'Well, I just wanted to congratulate your daughter on an incredible run.'

'Thank you.'

He turned back to Dina. 'How would you feel about joining our athletics club?'

'Blackheath and Bromley?'

'You're a bit too young for the big club just now, I'm afraid. But we could start you at the Bromley Bees.'

Dina looked at her parents.

'Mum? Dad?'

They both smiled at her. 'Well, it's your decision. Would you like to join?'

Dina nodded her head enthusiastically.

'Yes! I'd love to!'

Then a look of doubt crossed her face and she turned back to John. 'You won't make me do cross country, will you?!'

'You don't want to do it? Even though you're so good at it?'

'No! Never again.'

John laughed. 'Well I haven't seen you on field and track yet.'

He crossed his arms and looked at her with a twinkle in his eye. 'How do I know you're any good?'

Mrs Carty piped up, 'Oh, she is, I can tell you! Flies faster than the wind!'

'Well,' replied John, 'I look forward to working with you at The Bees.'

CHAPTER 5

OLYMPIC DREAMS

Dina felt her skin tingle. She watched Kelly Holmes prepare to settle into the starting block. She had a look of cool, calm concentration on her face as she stared down the track.

It was the 2004 Athens Olympics and Dina was so nervous that even her favourite hot chicken wings sat uneaten by her side. Kelly had been troubled by leg injuries in the year running up to the Olympics, but she was still favourite for the gold medal in the 800 metres. However, it would be a tight race against three-time world champion Maria de Lurdes Mutola. Kelly had never been able to beat her.

Eight-year-old Dina couldn't imagine what was going through Kelly's head as the gun fired for the start of the race. Kelly had come out of retirement and, at the age of 34, was giving the Olympics one last shot. The commentators and the whole of Britain were behind her. Just two minutes of running lay ahead of her but everyone knew how much winning a medal would mean to her.

Dina and her parents sat glued to the television as Kelly approached the final lap. She was still in last place, steadily striding behind eight other runners.

'She's trailing at the back at the moment but I don't think she will for much longer!' said the commentator, and Dina clung to their hopeful words.

'I can't watch!' Dina's mum fled the room.

'Oh, Julie, you can't miss her becoming an Olympic champion!' Dina's dad was optimistic.

'Just call me back in if she's doing well!'

'She's pacing, Mum, she's pacing!' Dina called after her. She knew how important this was in any long-distance race. She took her eyes off the screen for a second before turning back to watch Kelly, who began attacking on the outside, and gaining ground on her nemesis, Maria.

'She's in it, Julie – she's back in it!'

'What?!' Julie hurried back to the doorway of the lounge.

'Oh wow – would you look at that!' Kelly had levelled with world champions Hasna Benhassi and Jolanda Čeplak. They were just 50 metres from the finish and approaching the final bend.

'Come on Kelly – come on!' The three of them were up on their feet cheering her on with the crowd as she sped down the final lap to challenge Maria in the lead.

'It's so close!' cried Julie.

'She's gonna do it!' said Winston.

'Come on, Kelly!' Dina roared at the TV. She held her breath as she watched her battle to overtake Maria, Hasna still threatening from the outside. Then she leapt for joy as Kelly scraped the finishing line to take first place, with Hasna in second and Jolanda flying from behind to finish third.

'She's done it!'

'Just wonderful!'

'What a performance!'

The three of them jumped around and hugged each other.

It was one of the tightest 800-metre races for women in Olympic history. They saw a look of confusion pass over Kelly's face, because she was still unsure if she was first across the line. Tears filled Dina's eyes as the commentator screamed their congratulations at the top of their lungs, and she saw the pure elation on Kelly's face as she realised she'd taken gold for Britain.

Kelly had won by five hundredths of a second in a new world record time of 1 minute 56 seconds. Her long wait to be an Olympic champion was over and Dina had a new hero.

Five nights later Dina watched her fall to the ground in disbelief after she won the 1500 metres final with a personal best of 3 minutes 57 seconds. It was her second Olympic gold medal, achieved against the odds.

'Just incredible,' said Julie. 'The oldest woman to ever win either race, let alone both!'

'And the first British athlete to win a double Olympic gold in both races for 80 years!' said Winston.

Dina watched Kelly struggle to hold back her emotions as she stood on the podium wrapped in the British flag, her gold medal around her neck. When the British national anthem ended, she waved to the crowd. Dina was particularly captivated by the laurel wreath that Kelly was wearing. She looked just like the Greek goddesses she learnt about at school.

'You know, Mum, the wreath is a symbol of triumph! Apollo wore one! And it's what they always used to give to the athletes when they won!'

Julie replied: 'Looks as though it gets in the way a bit, though!' They both laughed as Kelly's wreath slipped down her forehead, momentarily distracting her.

Dina imagined how it would feel to stand on the highest platform of the podium, winning gold for Great Britain and waving to the crowds. And how cool it would be to wear a wreath! If this was the closest she could get to being a Greek goddess, she'd give it a shot! Whatever it took!

That night she took out some coloured crayons and drew a picture of herself upon an Olympic tri-level podium. It was an ordinary enough looking picture of her in sportswear, but there were two finishing touches. Firstly, she added a laurel wreath. She held it up, admiring her handiwork. Finally, she took a pen and wrote in capitals underneath: I WANT TO BE AN OLYMPIC CHAMPION.

CHAPTER 6

HOLDING THE HORSES

'It's Saturday!' Every weekend Dina leapt out of bed and threw on her black and orange Bromley Bees Academy kit and matching trainers. She was filled with excitement at the thought of another fun day at Norman Park Athletics Track.

As club founder, Mick Jones, explained to the children who attended the club, they were there to learn the basics of running, jumping and throwing to give them a broad exposure to athletics. One of Dina's favourite events was the long jump. As she pelted down the runway towards the sandpit, she loved the feeling of acceleration in her feet before she propelled herself forward.

'Wheeee!' she shouted, flying through the air with a huge smile on her face before she landed in the sand. It was the closest she came to feeling like she was flying. She was also good at it. As the weeks went by, her jumping distance grew from four to six feet, improving her personal best each time. Dina had also made friends with a girl called Shannon Hylton, who loved sprinting just as much as she did.

One Saturday, after she'd jumped nearly 10 feet, John drew her aside.

'Well, your teacher was right – you can definitely run!'

Dina beamed.

'But more specifically than that, I think you're a sprinter.' John was particularly impressed with the ground she could cover in a short space of time on the long-jump runway. Dina's heart soared at these words, just as it did when she flew down the track with the wind in her hair.

'How about we try you out in some 100- and 200-metre races with the other kids?'

Dina nodded enthusiastically.

Mick and John watched in amazement as she tore round the track, overtaking all the other children. Some were older than her and had been training at the club for several years.

Mick said: 'She's just so...'

'"Springy" is the only word I can think of,' said John.

'If she keeps progressing like this, she'll be through to the Blackheath and Bromley club in no time,' said John.

Mick turned to him. 'What do you think about coaching her, John? Think she's got the potential to go far?'

John paused for a moment. 'I think she's got it in her to go all the way,' he replied.

Mick looked surprised. 'I don't think I've seen you this sure about anyone for a long time.'

'Well, we'll have to see, of course. But my

instinct is that she's got the attitude to match her talent.'

'Olympic champion?'

'Quite possibly.'

Mick whistled. 'Well, if that's what you think, then we need to invest in her.'

After Dina crossed the finishing line, John beckoned her over. 'We're very impressed with how you've developed here. As well as your natural sprinting ability, you've got good agility, balance and coordination too.'

Dina smiled. 'Thank you,' she said.

'But,' John said quickly, 'do you want to become even faster?'

Dina nodded her head vigorously.

He continued. 'It's all good being naturally gifted, but about 70 per cent of speed is down to training and technique.'

'If you'd like to, I think we can take your training up to the next level. How would you feel about putting in some extra hours of coaching each week?

Here at the track, with me?'

Dina's eyes lit up. 'Yes please!'

'If your parents agree, we'll put together a plan to start working towards some national competitions.'

Dina's eyes widened. 'Really?'

'Yes, I think you're ready. Although I'll never push you to do anything I don't think you're ready for.'

'Are you going to get me pumping iron in the gym then?'

'Hmm, no, I'll go easy on you for now, you're still growing. Just some simple strength training using resistance bands.'

'That's what Apollo must have done, I reckon.'

'Ha! Well yes, the gods were pretty blessed in that way. They didn't have to work for their superhero powers, they just had them. But us mere mortals have to work for it!'

She thought of Kelly Holmes standing up on the podium and the picture she'd drawn. Was she prepared to work for it? She still enjoyed swimming and playing hockey every week. Would this take time away from that? Plus, it wasn't long until she started big school.

John read her mind. 'Now, I know your mum is a little concerned this might impact your homework when you start secondary school. What are your thoughts?'

Dina thought about it. She loved athletics but she also loved learning. She would find a way.

She nodded determinedly and said: 'I can do both.'

John smiled. 'That's what I thought. You're not one to hold the horses.'

'Hold the what?'

He laughed. 'Don't hold the horses. It's one of my favourite phrases. You'll find out soon enough.'

CHAPTER 7

DARREN CAMPBELL

Dina gazed out towards the field she'd run around on sports day and down the road towards Poverest Park. It was her last day at Perry Hall Primary before she moved to secondary school and she wanted to soak up the childhood memories.

'Dina!' Nicole's voice brought her back to earth. 'You haven't signed my jumper yet!' Nicole headed towards her, her school jumper covered in scrawls and signatures. 'I definitely want yours! It'll be worth a fortune one day when you're an Olympic champion!'

Dina laughed. 'Well, if that does happen, I'll

have you to thank, I suppose!' She thought back to the day in Poverest Park when Nicole bought her an ice cream.

'Oh, whatever!' said Nicole. Dina's humility always amazed her.

Miss Hudson and Mrs Carty gave Dina a big goodbye hug. She struggled to hold back the tears. There were so many happy memories from her school and these teachers, the first to encourage her running, were still so supportive:

'You're going to love it there. You'll be doing big proper history lessons now, where you'll get to learn about more than just the Ancient Greeks. You'll be a fountain of knowledge before long.'

'Yes, you'll know more than us in no time!'

'Now, we don't want you to come back and see us till you're a big running star, okay?'

Dina nodded through the tears. 'I promise.'

***

'He's here!' Dina announced excitedly to her classmates. They scrambled from their seats and gathered at the window to see Olympic champion Darren Campbell arrive at the gates of her secondary school, Newstead Wood. He was one of the four sprinters who'd won gold for Great Britain in the 4 x 100 metres relay race in Athens 2004; they were a dream team who had demonstrated just how technically brilliant the skill of baton passing could be. Dina couldn't believe it. She'd watched him run the second leg on the TV over four years earlier and now in 2008 he was here: an Olympic gold medallist visiting their school.

Darren was visiting on behalf of the Youth Sports Trust to announce a new partnership he'd founded with Olympic champion Todd Bennett, called the Team Superschools project. Together, they planned to visit over two thousand schools before the 2012 London Olympics to introduce children to the basics of athletics. Before they took on a variety of physical challenges and warm-ups in the school hall, Darren spoke to Dina's class.

He looked ordinary enough in a white sports T-shirt, but Dina's prepared questions for him soon disappeared from her mind as he grinned at the class and began to speak in a rich Mancunian accent.

'Who managed to watch any of the Beijing Olympic Games coverage this summer?'

'Me!' Everyone threw their hands up.

'And why's the next one so special?'

They all replied in unison: 'Because it's in London!'

'Our capital city!'

They all nodded.

'Did anyone see Jessica Ennis take bronze in the 100 metres hurdles last year at the European Championships in Hungary?'

Dina nodded her head vigorously. She loved the British athlete and was enjoying watching her career unfold.

'Anyone know what her time was?'

Dina stuck her hand up and shouted out: 'It was 13.1 seconds!'

Darren smiled broadly. 'Excellent! You must be a fan.'

'I am!'

'Well, she'll be wanting to beat that time at the next Olympics. And I think she's on track to take gold next time. Four years. Seems like a long time away, right?'

The class nodded.

'But the champions we will see at 2012 are all working towards it now. We just won't get to see how hard they're working. We won't see the failures, the false starts, the tears or disappointments and injuries, we'll just see the results of all the hard work they put in. I was lucky enough to train with my coach Linford Christie six days a week in the years leading up to our relay team's success in 2004. Without that hard work we wouldn't have beaten the American team. And in this game, split seconds count. We beat them by just 0.01 seconds in a season's best of 38.07 seconds.'

The Olympics did seem eons away to 12-year-old Dina too, but she knew that the work she was doing now with John was building up her strength and endurance for her own athletic goals. She'd progressed to Blackheath and Bromley and was now training for eight hours a week at their training ground.

From planks to push-ups and squats, Dina worked on slowly building up her core strength along with running sets of 100 metres at race pace with two-minute breaks in between. In the summer of 2009 she came second in the 100 metres at the Blackheath and Bromley Open at a personal best of 13.4 seconds. She wanted to shave at least a second off in time for the Kent Schools Championships the following summer.

As John explained to her, their aim was to concentrate on her personal bests rather than worry about always being the fastest in the race.

'We need to work towards you comfortably

beating your own targets,' he said, 'rather than focusing on who the fastest is in the race, the county or even the country. You don't have to be the best, but I do expect you to commit to being your best.'

As a budding athlete of the school, Dina was picked to show Darren around the school's track and field facilities later in the afternoon. Her nerves subsided a little and she began to share her hopes to compete in the European Championships one day. When Dina's mother came to collect her from school she was chatting away excitedly to the Olympic medallist.

As soon as she spotted her mum, Dina rushed over to her.

'Mum – could you take a photo of us?' She looked back at Darren and asked him: 'If that's okay?'

'Yes, of course!' Darren replied.

Darren had brought in his Olympic gold medal and asked Dina if she'd like to hold it.

She held the medal in her hands. 'It feels heavy!'

Darren laughed. 'I should think so, there's meant to be at least six grams of gold in it!'

Dina thought how wonderful it must be for him to keep something like that, as a continual reminder of his achievement. She hoped she could feel the weight of a gold medal around her neck one day. She held it up to the camera and smiled.

Then Darren asked her: 'Dina, would you like to wear it?' It was as if he'd read her mind.

Dina's eyes lit up. 'Really?'

'Of course!'

She went to put it around her neck, but her mother stepped forward quickly to stop her.

'Ah, no, the first medal Dina wears will be her own.'

Dina felt her cheeks flush. Trust Mum to tell an Olympic champion what to do.

'Mum...' she muttered under her breath.

Darren nodded his head in approval.

'No, your mum's right. I remember thinking something very similar when I was around your age. That's a good mindset to have.'

Dina smiled, although she was still a little embarrassed.

'Do you want to have your own medal, Dina?' asked Darren.

Without a moment's hesitation, she replied: 'Yes.'

Darren looked into her determined eyes. He could see she meant it.

He turned to Dina's mother.

'As part of the launch for the Youth Sports Trust,' he said, 'we're handing out grants to help young athletes. I think Dina should apply.'

Julie smiled as Darren turned back to Dina and said: 'Whatever your dreams are, believe in them, because they can come true.'

As soon as Dina got home, she began work on her grant application with her mother. Together, they went through the list of questions. Towards the end, Dina was asked to provide a short personal statement. She thought long and hard for a minute before answering: 'I don't have to be *the* best but

I'm determined to show up and be *my* best.'

A few weeks later, Dina and her parents had something to celebrate. She'd been awarded a bursary to help towards training gear, sportswear and equipment.

Dina was very happy. It felt great to know that some world champions believed she was worth the investment. She thought back to the words Darren had left her with: 'Whatever your dreams are, believe in them, because they can come true.'

A few weeks later, Dina injured her foot in a hockey match and had to stop playing any sport to rest and recover. She desperately missed keeping active, but it helped her decide on the sport she most wanted to concentrate on. Out of all of them, she missed running the most. She was determined, more than ever, to make it her main focus.

CHAPTER 8

RECORD-BREAKER

11 July 2009

It was a warm day for the Aviva English Schools Athletics Championships. Dina stood in lane three as she prepared for the Junior Girls 4 x 100 metres relay race and took in the sheer size of the Don Valley Stadium in Sheffield. She quashed the urge to break out into a Beyoncé dance routine to control her nerves – a trick which usually worked in the call-up room, much to John's bewilderment.

Don Valley was surely the largest stadium where she'd competed so far, and in one of the biggest competitions. Her team weren't just running for their school, they were running for their county, Kent, and were up against seven others that included Lancashire, Manchester and West Yorkshire.

Dina had had a lot of fun practising with her relay team. Georgina Middleton had been chosen to lead the race. Dina herself would tackle the longest back straight on the second, before passing to Sophie Ayre. Rhiannon Jones would take the last leg.

Dina thought of her parents in the crowd. She knew her mum would be videoing her performance from start to finish. Her times had got steadily faster throughout the year; from her 12.9-second 100 metres at the Kent Schools Championships in April, to 12.8 seconds a month later. She knew she could make a difference to the race.

She was getting better at controlling her nerves before each race. In fact, she rather enjoyed them. She remembered a word of advice that Darren Campbell had given them in the talk at school: 'You need the heartbeat. But you need to control it.'

She knew the nerves would be building in the rest of the team as they stood in their positions around the track, waiting for what felt like an eternity before the start. They'd practised their handovers as often as they possibly could but there was little time or funding to perfect them.

Dina felt a surge of excitement as she heard the muffled tones of the announcer over the tannoy. 'On your marks...'

She always thought of John's words – 'Don't hold the horses' – while she did her final few jumps to warm up and anticipated the start of the race.

'Get set...' Dina's heart raced as she waited for the gun to fire.

Bang!

They blasted out of the blocks. West Yorkshire started well and soon took the lead while Georgina trailed in fourth behind. Dina knew she and the rest of the Kent team had some catching up to do. As Georgina drew close, Dina began the run for the handover. Once she took the baton, she flew down the back straight, her legs pounding, staring determinedly ahead to Sophie, who held her hand out behind her. West Yorkshire were still in the lead but the changeover between Dina and Sophie was seamless.

'Go Sophie, go!' Dina cheered her on and watched with delight as she gained ground on the inside to overtake West Yorkshire and Norfolk. On the final bend she took the lead before she handed to Rhiannon, who raced down the final stretch.

Now Kent had the lead.

But it wasn't their time to take gold. In the last 10 metres, West Yorkshire and Norfolk closed in steadily on Rhiannon, leaving her to trail home in third place. However, the Kent team were happy to pick up bronze.

'Yay! We got a medal!'

Dina was hailed as the star of the team, who'd helped them claw back from fourth place on the second leg.

'I don't think we could have got ahead without

you, Dina.'

'You absolutely tore down that track.'

Dina protested, 'But, guys, it was a team effort!'

'You were born to sprint!'

That summer, the medals kept coming for Dina in her personal races. In August, she took gold in the 100 metres at the England Under 17 and Under 15 Championships at Bedford Stadium, the same month that she won the same event at the SEAA Under 15 and Under 20 Inter Counties Match in Watford.

Yet, despite these successes, Dina was a little frustrated that her times weren't improving significantly. They continued to hover around the 12.10 and 12.12 second mark and were slower than some of her earlier runs in the year.

She discussed her concern with John. 'I thought runners were meant to get faster in the summer!'

John reassured her. 'Sometimes this happens after a year of hard training. I know you want to be faster but if we push your body any harder we could cause too much stress on your muscles, which we don't want to do. It's important to pace yourself. Continue to do the work and the faster times will come.'

He added: 'Dina, right now, you're winning most of your races but that won't be the case when you start competing in bigger events. On the European or international stage it may take you time to pick up a medal; for now, you could be coming in fourth or fifth.'

The thought of coming fourth in any race seemed bizarre to Dina, but she trusted John and knew he always had her best interests at heart.

'If you want to be a champion,' he said, 'you need to be able to accept that and not give up. We go at the pace that's right for you, okay?'

She nodded.

Yet, in early August, Dina achieved a personal best of 39.16 seconds in the 300 metres at the Tonbridge Avril Bowring Open. It was a vast improvement on her time of 44.37 seconds earlier that year.

***

Dina flopped down in front of the TV and tucked into her favourite pepperoni pizza to celebrate. As she savoured each mouthful, she overheard her mother on the phone to John.

'The fastest what? Really?! That's amazing news! Thank you, John.'

A few seconds later she peered around the door of the lounge. 'Guess what, Dina? You're a record-breaker!'

'What?'

'No other 13-year-old has ever run that fast in a 300-metre race!'

'In the country?'

'In the world!'

Dina's mouth fell open.

'Isn't that fantastic?'

'Yes!'

Dina couldn't believe it. She was a record-breaker. And suddenly the thought of breaking more records seemed possible.

'I think this could be the first of many,' said her mother.

CHAPTER 9

HARD WORK PAYS OFF

'Head up! Chest up! Keep your knees bent!'

The autumn nights were drawing in and it was getting colder out on the track at Norman Park. John had increased her training to four times a week ahead of the English Schools' Championships the following summer. It was her dream to win the Championships in either the 100 or 200 metres with a new personal best. Her 200 was currently 25 seconds and they were both working on reducing that.

John began setting new exercises for Dina to improve her overall fitness, which included jumps, hops and skips. As Dina practised jumping up on to a bench in the gym, John explained why they were important.

'When you exert maximum force on your muscles in a short space of time, it will help to increase their power and strength.'

'You'd better be right, John,' Dina groaned, as she struggled to regain her breath after her fourth round of 10 jumps.

John smiled. 'I am. You'll be even more springy in no time.'

Dina sighed. She knew the workouts were important, but they weren't as much fun as just racing down the track. 'It's a bit boring, John. Can I listen to some music when I do it?' She loved to work out to Jay-Z.

John shook his head. 'It's important to maintain absolute focus when you do these exercises. If you get distracted you might use your muscles in the wrong way or do some damage.'

Dina was normally very tired when she returned

home from a long day of school and training. She was often tempted to flop out on the sofa and catch up on the latest reality TV show before bed. But she knew that wasn't an option now. She looked at the homework schedule she'd drawn up to help her juggle schoolwork and training.

Dina had also recently picked her GCSE subjects. She still loved history as much as she had in primary school and was looking forward to studying it in more detail.

After studying from half nine to ten for a maths test the next day, and downing a banana smoothie snack made by her mum, Dina settled down to bed. She was asleep the second her head hit the pillow. The next day she would follow the same routine all over again. It was a tough schedule to stick to throughout the whole of the winter, but she had a temporary break at Christmas, vegging out in front of the TV watching movies, eating ice cream and chicken drumsticks. She vowed to return to training in the new year, in preparation for the summer championships.

Dina's hard work would pay off. Throughout early 2010 she excelled, winning almost every single 100- and 200-metre race she entered. In June she won the 200 metres at the Kent Schools Championships in 24.73 seconds.

'You can run it faster than this,' said John.

'I know,' she said in frustration.

'Don't waste your time beating yourself up about it, though. Conserve as much energy as possible ahead of the English Schools' Championships. We've got another four weeks to work on it. So do your best to avoid any drama going on at school, relax, watch movies – and no over-exerting yourself with any dance routines!'

Dina laughed. 'But they help me let off steam!'

'We need that steam for the track!'

Dina continued to train hard but took off one or two days a week to catch up on movies and relax with friends. It was nearly the summer holidays and classes were winding down a little after their end-of-year exams. One evening, she came to training in a more subdued mood than usual.

'What's up?' asked John, not used to seeing her like this.

'Has something happened at school?'

She shook her head.

'No, I just watched *The Notebook*! Oh John, it's so sad.' Her eyes began to well up.

'Oh no!' said John. 'When I said "Relax and watch movies" maybe I should have specified... don't watch anything that's going to upset you! You need all the energy you can get! From now on – no more tearjerkers! And definitely no scary movies!'

CHAPTER 10

A RISING STAR

9 July 2010

It was another warm July day and the final of
the 200 metres at the next Aviva English Schools
Championships, this time in Birmingham. Dina
was both nervous and excited as she took in the size
of the Alexander Stadium. All her races throughout
the year had built up to this and she couldn't wait
to fly down the track.

She felt like a rocket waiting for lift-off as she
stretched and jumped up and down on the spot to
warm up her muscles. She'd won the heat earlier
that day in a time of 25 seconds, but she wanted

to beat that – so John's theory seemed to have worked. She thought of him in the crowd, watching with her parents. She knew they got just as nervous as she did before a race, but there was nothing they could do to help as they watched from the stands. In the end, it was always down to her to run the race well.

She glanced briefly at the other competitors. She remembered John's warning. 'Never become complacent enough to think that you're the best because anything can happen in athletics. Don't give someone the chance to be better than you.'

She looked down at the shoes her mum had recently bought her to replace the pair she purchased when she received her sports grant. That felt like a long time ago now. She smiled again as a shot of excitement ran through her. She wasn't going to let them down.

'On your marks...'

Dina jumped up and down one last time as she settled into the starting blocks.

'Get set...'

Bang!

It was a good start for Dina and she used the bend to her advantage to take the lead. The noise of the crowd blended into the background as she focused on lifting her knees and legs as high as she could, speeding down the last 60 metres. No one had a chance to close in on her as she flew out in front, her arms outstretched as she crossed the finishing line. A huge smile broke out on to her face as she checked her time on the clock: 24.93 seconds. She'd won. But more importantly, she'd beaten her previous personal best.

A month later, Dina won a gold medal in the 100 metres at the Aviva England Athletics Championships in Bedford. She ran a personal best of 12.00 seconds, beating her previous time of 12.21 seconds in an event two months earlier. Dina's confidence was growing all the time and she felt even more ready to take on international events.

As the summer drew to a close, John discussed

upcoming events with her. 'I think you're ready to compete at the next European Youth Olympics. How'd you like to go to Turkey next year?'

Dina's face lit up as she heard the word 'Olympics'.

'Oh, John, I'd love to!'

'Great.'

'Hang on, does that mean...?'

'Yes, you'll be representing Great Britain. This will be your first British vest!'

Dina pictured herself holding up the Union Jack as she ran the lap of honour. Her heart skipped a beat at the thought of running for her country. She was another step closer to becoming an Olympic champion.

***

The following summer, 2011, in Turkey, Dina once more thought of that vision of herself, draped in the Union Jack, in her mind as she settled into the blocks. She stared down the track two metres ahead of her and focused her mind. She was about to run in the final of the 200 metres at the European Youth Olympics. She'd performed well in the last two heats, coming in first and second place to qualify. In under 30 seconds' time, would she win a medal for Britain? Silence descended upon the Hüseyin Avni Aker Stadium.

'Set!' Dina put her head down, straightened her back and raised her body. She held her breath as she waited for the gun.

Bang!

Dina sprang out of the blocks but ran to a crashing halt when two shots were fired into the air. All the runners looked around accusingly at each other. One of them must have made a false start. Dina felt her cheeks grow hotter and her hands start to sweat as the event adjudicator walked towards her with a stern expression on their face. She felt a deep sense of shame in the pit of her stomach as she realised she was the one who had made a mistake. As her cheeks grew hotter, she began to walk off the track, and back towards the athletes' call-up room. She felt someone pat her on the shoulder and gently say her name.

'Dina, are you okay?' It was Jo Jennings, the former English high-jump champion, who was also development manager for British Athletics.

'I'm fine,' replied Dina. She did her best to keep her head held high, although she knew she was on the verge of tears.

'Don't cry here,' she told herself.

As she entered the call-up room she looked at the concerned faces of John and her parents, who ran over to comfort her.

'I'm sorry!' she said, before she burst into floods of tears. She felt absolutely devastated. The heats had gone so well but she'd ruined her chances of becoming a champion in a split second.

'There, there,' said John, 'you won't be the first or last athlete to make a false start. Happens to the best of them – even Linford Christie, wouldn't you know?'

Dina tried to get her words out through her tears. 'I can't believe it, I've failed – failed!'

'Dina, you are human. You will make mistakes sometimes, I'm afraid.'

'But I don't want to make mistakes!'

'It's part of this process. This one mistake today will mean you'll probably never make another false start again in your life.'

'You think so?'

'Yes. You will improve because of this. You will become a better runner. I know it.'

The uncomfortable sensation began to ease in Dina's stomach a little. She'd had John as her coach long enough to know she could trust him.

John continued. 'You need to take away the positives from today. Number one, you're good enough to compete internationally. Number two, you've beaten your personal best in the 200 metres. And number three, most importantly of all, your mascara hasn't run.'

Dina mustered a smile. She'd got into the habit of applying eye make-up before each of her runs, obstinately telling John: 'I like make-up. Besides, I want to look ready for the cameras if I win a race.' The plaits were long gone too, replaced with a more mature and sleek bun.

Dina felt awful but she knew deep down that John was right. Something good would come from this.

'This is part of the process,' John had told her, 'of going from junior to senior. I know you've got it in you to make that jump.'

Dina vowed there and then to keep going and to work on her starts out of the blocks to ensure she never made another false start again. On the flight back home, she was already looking ahead to 2012. It was going to be an important year. Not just for London, when all eyes of the world would be on the city, but for Dina, who would be sitting her GCSEs and training to compete in the World Junior Athletics Championships.

CHAPTER 11

THE END OF
AN ERA

Dina and her friends raced to the top of Poverest Park. They'd just taken their last GCSE exam and were thrilled to be out of hot and stuffy exam rooms for good. Temperatures across the country had been soaring.

They all shouted at the top of their lungs: 'No more exams!'

They proceeded to roll back down the hill laughing and giggling, just like they had when they were kids. This was going to be a special summer. Not just because they'd finished their GCSEs but because London was hosting the Summer

Olympics. The 2012 logo was emblazoned across posters and billboards across Orpington, and the capital's other surrounding towns and boroughs, along with the faces of the sporting heroes the country was pinning their hopes on: Jessica Ennis, Mo Farah, Greg Rutherford. The event that Darren Campbell had talked about so excitedly, all those years ago in her school classroom, was finally upon them.

Dina knew, though, that she couldn't switch off completely over that summer. While her friends talked excitedly about the upcoming school prom, where they were going on holiday and how they planned to celebrate, her mind kept drifting off to what was ahead of her. Within a month she'd be in Barcelona. Not for a holiday, not for relaxation – but to compete in the World Junior Athletics Championships.

She sighed as she saw her friends tuck into their second tub of ice cream each, and said, 'It's torture to watch you eat that.'

'Can't you just have a bit?'

'It wouldn't just be a bit. Anyway, I promised John. And he told me I can have as much as I want – after I've won a medal! I'm telling you now, the afternoon of the fifteenth of July... I've got a date with a whole vanload of the stuff, I don't care what he says!'

They all laughed.

'You've got such discipline, Dina, I couldn't stick to it.'

'Yeah, it's worth it.'

'You'll smash it, Dina.'

'Well, that's not very likely,' said Dina. 'I'm competing on a world stage. I'm up against some great runners from the USA and Jamaica. For once, I think I'll be watching their backsides fly ahead of me.'

'You could get a medal for modesty, Dina.'

'No, honestly, if I do well enough in the 200 metre heats to qualify for the finals, I'll be really happy. And beat my personal best, of course.'

'What do you need to get to achieve that?'

'Shave off at least a second.'

'Just a second?'

Dina laughed. 'Remember, Kelly Holmes won by one five hundreth of a second. Seconds don't count in a race, hundreths of a second count!'

'You're up there with the best of them Dina, that's what counts.'

She smiled. 'We'll see.'

CHAPTER 12

PERSONAL BEST

13 July 2012

Dina took one last look around the Estadi Olímpic Lluís Companys stadium in Barcelona as she prepared for the 200 metres final. This was the stadium where the 1992 Olympics had taken place, three years before she was even born. She was standing on the same track where champions Steve Redgrave and Linford Christie had wowed the world with their outstanding performances. She gave herself a moment to take it all in.

In comparison, how important was her run? She shook her head and smiled. Hadn't Allyson Felix, a runner she'd admired for years, broken a record in these Championships eight years before?

No – Dina reasoned that she might not be an elite champion just yet, but she was heading in the right direction and about to achieve something incredible in her own right, if she could focus and get a handle on the butterflies churning in her stomach.

She had performed outstandingly in the 200 metres qualifiers earlier in the day, bringing in times that improved with each heat: from 23.71 seconds down to 23.57 seconds. These times were currently not that far behind the USA's Dezerea Bryant at 23.11 or the Bahamas' Anthonique Strachan at 23.28.

The gun fired and the athletes tore off down the track. It was clear from the start that Anthonique had made an incredible start, exploding out of the blocks like a bullet, with Dezerea and Olivia Ekpone of the USA hot on her heels. Dina concentrated on running as fast as she could but she couldn't catch up with them and trailed behind, something that was still so new to her. She saw Anthonique cross the finishing line to win a record-breaking gold at 22.53 seconds. Olivia and Dezerea followed neck-and-neck behind her to take silver and bronze.

Dina crossed the line in seventh place but as she checked the clock her heart skipped a beat. Despite her placing, she'd achieved a new personal best: 23.50.

'Yes!' She punched the air with her fists and threw her hands up to her face as relief washed over her.

'Well done, Dina.' She heard John's calm voice behind her. He was never one to get carried away with emotion. She glanced over at the British runner Desirèe Henry who'd come in fourth. Dina knew she'd be disappointed, just as she was, not to win a place on the podium. But, deep down, Dina knew that if she kept working on improving her times, one day she would.

Dina was taken aback when the press began

to gather around her and fire questions. She was beginning to look like a hot new sporting hope for Britain.

'With a performance like that, Dina, do you feel hopeful for the European Junior Championships next year?'

Dina smiled politely and nodded. 'Yes, I'm looking forward to them.'

But in all honesty, there was only one thing on her mind right then.

She turned to John. 'I'd kill for some ice cream!'

'Yeah, I think you deserve it.'

The taste of vanilla ice cream melting in her mouth had never felt so good. She was elated. She had made the 200 metres final and achieved a new PB.

CHAPTER 13

LONDON 2012

Dina felt the hairs on the back of her neck go up as she entered the Olympic Stadium. The sound of 80,000 excited and expectant home crowd fans echoed around the arena. In every direction that Dina looked there was a sign or banner in support of the British athletes performing that day.

It was Saturday, 4 August 2012 and Dina, along with her friend Shannon and other athletes from Blackheath and Bromley, had all been chosen to be box carriers, which meant they had the job of carrying kit for the competing British Olympic athletes. Initially, Dina had been disappointed she wasn't chosen for the following day, when Usain Bolt was running. But, already, they could sense they were about to witness something magical that day.

As Dina made her way to the call-up room with the other volunteers, her hands began to tremble slightly. She knew she had to focus on her job but it was difficult not to get distracted.

'I can't believe it!' Shannon hissed under her breath. 'I'm carrying Mo Farah's shorts! He could become an Olympic champion in these today!'

She looked at Dina, who started giggling.

'Dina, I'm serious. I'm not sure I can do it! What if I get so overwhelmed I faint and drop his box?!'

'You'd better let me carry it then, if you're not up to the job!'

'No way!' They began to squabble over who should be tasked with this great honour.

But as they walked into the call-up room, they felt not only the weight of the boxes they carried but the weight of pressure and responsibility each athlete was feeling.

Dina was glad that John had chosen her to volunteer. This was a great opportunity to see and feel what it was like to compete on a world stage, as well as to experience the added pressure of performing to a home crowd, who so desperately wanted you to win.

The tension was almost unbearable. Despite the din awaiting them outside, there was barely any sound in the room as the athletes paced up and down, warmed up their muscles or spoke in muffled tones to their coaches, whose expressions gave away little of their own feelings.

Darren's words from four years earlier returned to Dina as she watched Mo Farah, Greg Rutherford and Jessica Ennis prepare for the biggest challenges of their careers to date. Few of the spectators would know of the struggles or pains they'd overcome to reach that competitive level. Nor could they comprehend just how nervous they were.

This was a revelation for Dina. Here she was,

just a few feet from some of the most talented athletes in the world, athletes who were probably about to make Olympic history. Yet even these revered sporting heroes got nervous. It reassured her somehow. Yes, she thought, everyone gets nervous. But it's about how you work with your nerves, rather than allowing them to control you. She thought about the races she had run and each race she would run in the future. She vowed to herself there and then: 'Rather than battling my own nerves, I'll accept they'll always exist and work with them to propel me forward.'

At the edge of the track, Dina was close enough to watch a series of emotions cross Jessica's face as she waited to run the 800 metres, her final event, in lane eight; emotions of doubt, anxiety, dread and fear. They were all there. Dina couldn't imagine the pressure she was feeling in that moment. She was in first place in the heptathlon event, but the gold medal rested on her performance in the 800 metres. Jess knew that if she ran it in a time that was close to her best, no other runner could catch her. In second place was the Lithuanian athlete Austra Skujytė, but this race wasn't Austra's strongest event. Could the Ukraine's Lyudmyla Yosypenko cover enough ground to catch her?

Dina gripped the hands of her fellow box carriers as they all held their breath and watched from the side of track eight, waiting for the gun to fire. Could the World Champion take gold for her country in front of a home crowd? Jess got a good start out of the blocks and comfortably took the lead in the first 400-metre lap. It looked as though she had the race wrapped up. As the bell for the final lap rang Dina felt Shannon's grip on her arm tighten. Jess was still in the lead. But then, in the final 300 metres, she faced fresh challenges as three competitors passed her – one included Tatyana Chernova. Dina and the other volunteers began to pace up and down to work off their nervous energy.

Dina could hardly bear to watch as the support from the crowd reached new heights, with cries of 'Come on, Jess!' and 'Bring it back!' The entire stadium was cheering Jess on to win, helping to provide the energy she needed to fight the last part of this battle.

They watched in amazement as Jess turned the corner of the final lap and clawed her way back. With a sudden burst of speed, she overtook the athletes ahead of her and took on the home straight. The noise of the crowd was almost deafening as she took a clear lead. No one could get close to her now. Victory was in sight. She crossed the line and stretched out her arms before she fell to the ground and allowed her tears to flow. The crowd erupted.

Celebrating with her friends on the sidelines, Dina could feel the sense of joy and pride sweep around the stadium. They all knew how much it meant to Jess to win. Her disappointment at Beijing in 2008 and the injuries that had held her back all melted away in that moment. She'd overcome them all to succeed. It was her destiny to take gold that Saturday in front of an 80,000-strong home crowd who could share in that victory.

Suddenly, Dina's own destiny seemed clear to her, as the celebrations continued to reverberate around the stadium and indeed, the entire city of London. Dina was inspired, not only by Jess's physical strength but her determination to overcome her nerves and do battle with the doubt and uncertainty in her mind. She felt certain that she could incite the same feelings of joy and pride in people too. Just from running in a straight line. She laughed for a moment at the simplicity of it all. But there was a deep sense of certainty within her that this was what she wanted to do.

Jess struggled to hold back the tears on the podium as she collected her gold medal – the first athletics gold of the 2012 Olympics for Great Britain – and held it up to the roaring crowd. Afterwards, she wrapped herself in the Olympic Champion flag and an interviewer asked her how she felt. Dina watched as a huge smile broke out over her face when she answered: 'It just doesn't feel real.

To have all this support and to win in London is incredible.'

But the celebrations for Great Britain were not over yet. Dina watched from the sidelines again while a huge cheer went up for Mo Farah. He was the hot favourite to win the 10,000-metre race but with 25 laps to run and 27 other athletes competing, everyone knew it would be no mean feat. Ten minutes in, and with eighteen laps to go, Shannon joined Dina to watch his progress.

'Where is he?' They both scanned the track for his dark blue shorts.

'There he is!'

'He's really far behind!' Shannon groaned.

'It's early days,' said Dina. She knew from her cross-country days that he was pacing. 'He's got time to move in for the attack yet.'

Dina's words proved to be right. They watched, spellbound, as Mo started to move slowly and surely up the field.

'He's getting into position!' Dina shouted. The

excited roars from the crowd showed no signs of abating. They had energy enough for Mo too. Twenty minutes in and Mo was in seventh place with the USA's Galen Rupp and Ethiopia's Kenenisa Bekele steaming ahead.

But Dina knew all the athletes would have to look out for the Farah sprint.

'Look!' cried Dina as they watched him steadily move in on the attack. 'He's chasing Bekele!'

Then, with four laps to go, they watched Mo take the lead for the first time.

Dina and Shannon jumped up and down in excitement. But his fight was far from over as the other athletes continued to challenge and take the lead. With just over one lap to go, the runners bunched together, and everyone waited with bated breath. Who would make the first move to break free?

Then, as the bell rang for the final lap, they saw Mo take the lead, breaking into a long sprint. Bekele and Rupp were hot on his heels, but they were clearly struggling to keep up with him as he continued to increase his lead on the home straight. Could he take another gold medal for Britain that day?

'He's done it!' Dina and Shannon leapt up and down as they watched him cross the finish line and fall to the ground and kiss it.

What a night for Britain! Tears of pride ran down Dina's face as she watched Mo's overjoyed wife and daughter make their way down from the crowd to celebrate with him.

It wasn't the last British win of the day though. Greg Rutherford leapt 8.1 metres to take gold in the long jump. What an unbelievable day.

The news of Britain's success was splashed across the papers the next morning. The overjoyed faces of the Olympic champions were emblazoned across the front pages, along with the headline: 'Super Saturday'. Dina couldn't believe she'd been a part of one of the greatest days in British sporting history. She knew it had changed her life forever.

A few weeks later Dina had another reason to celebrate. But it had nothing to do with sport.

'Just tell me I've passed!' Dina covered her eyes while her mum logged onto the school system to find out Dina's exam results.

'Darling, you've done more than pass.'

Dina uncovered her eyes. 'You've got 10 A*s!'

Dina leapt around for joy. It was the perfect way to end a magical summer. She was heading into the sixth form to study A-levels in Biology, History and Politics.

CHAPTER 14

TRAINING HARD

Dina and Shannon danced around the kitchen, singing along to a Jay-Z song. It was the last day of the Christmas holidays and they were relaxing before the hard work resumed back at school and in training; Shannon was now also coached by John.

Dina sighed at the thought of returning to the hard grind. She'd been used to juggling schoolwork and training for years, but the pace had gone up a gear in the last term. As well as adjusting to A-levels, she was training for the European Athletics Junior Championships in Italy in Summer 2013. After her time off, she felt sluggish and demotivated.

She told her mum: 'This is the problem with winter. I love Christmas but I dread going back out on the track again after time off. I'll have slowed down like a right tortoise, I bet you!'

Dina had the London Under 20/Senior Games coming up at Lee Valley and admitted that she was a bit concerned about the 60-metre race she was running at the end of January.

Her mum knew she always strove to beat her personal bests, but she could see she wasn't her usual, energetic self.

'Dina, I think you need an incentive.'

Dina's ears pricked up. 'Oh yeah?'

'What was your last PB on the 60 metres?'

'7.48 seconds.'

Dina had run it at Crystal Palace the month before.

'Okay, if you get that down to 7.40 seconds by the end of January, I'll buy you a phone.'

Dina's eyes lit up. She loved a challenge and

needed one most during the long dark days in January.

'Mum, you're on!'

They shook hands on the bet.

From 7.48 to 7.40 seconds? Surely it was possible? She thought of the great Usain Bolt, who could cover 20 metres in just 1.61 seconds, and she smiled. It still amazed her the difference each hundredth of a second could make.

A few weeks after the race at Lee Valley, Dina arrived home to find a gift waiting for her on the kitchen table. She beamed. She knew exactly what it was. She'd won the 60 metres in a new personal best of 7.36, beating the time she'd originally set with her mum. Her local paper interviewed her for a piece highlighting the challenges of clocking incredible speeds while still tackling schoolwork and training.

It felt like another turning point for Dina. Since the 2012 Olympics, she had begun to feel that a career in athletics was not just highly likely but inevitable, and was looking ahead to the next Summer Olympics in 2016.

She told the press: 'I've got my heart set on Rio now. If you'd asked me a year ago, I don't think I would have believed it was possible. But I'm taking it more seriously now.'

She spent up to eight hours a week on the track with John, who could see that she wasn't taking the responsibility of being one of Britain's top sprinters lightly.

'If I relax,' she said, 'I give someone else the chance to beat me, John. You've always said that athletics is a sport where anyone can come out of nowhere.'

But history, particularly modern history, was still a strong passion of hers and she continued to work hard throughout the first year of her A-levels. While she trained with John, she would reel off fascinating facts about the European dictators during World War Two before rushing home to finish an essay on them.

As John would watch her leave, he often wondered how she maintained the stamina to juggle both athletics and her studies. But he knew that the standards Dina set herself in both areas were equally high. Success in one field often seeped into the other. Her confidence at school increased when she exceeded targets on the track.

As she worked towards completing her mock exams that summer, she continued to beat her personal bests. On 6 July in Birmingham she won the English Schools Championships 200 metres in a time of 23.63 seconds, despite racing into a strong headwind on the home straight.

John told her: 'Keep going like this, Dina, and you'll fly at the Junior Championships.'

Dina looked at him, bemused. It wasn't like John to praise her in this way. But she knew they both felt confident she could beat her personal best again in Italy.

Dina was extremely excited about Italy for a number of reasons. Not only did she have the opportunity to compete against some of Europe's fastest athletes but she was taking part in the 4 x 100 metres relay with three other athletes from Great Britain: Desirèe Henry, Yasmin Miller and Steffi Wilson. She always enjoyed relays because they were a chance to work on the same team with runners she admired and so often competed against.

Dina and Desirèe had become good friends during their practice for the relay, so Dina knew they'd both be grateful their relay took place after the sprints. However, any uncomfortable feelings about competing against her friend disappeared as she laid eyes on the small town of Reiti where the Championships took place. For a moment, she was too distracted by Romanesque churches and turreted houses perched upon snow-capped mountains. It occurred to her how fortunate she was to visit such beautiful European cities because of sport.

The day of the final for the 200 metres arrived. Dina was hopeful she could beat her personal best despite the heat in the stadium. 'Keep your personal best in mind and the rest will follow,' John always said. She would come first in the heats, but she knew she still faced stiff competition from Desirèe and Tessa van Schagen, who weren't far behind her with their own personal bests. It would be a close race.

Tackling the bend was often the trickiest part of the race for Dina, because she tended to tighten up on it, and so she remembered the techniques she'd worked on with John: 'Tilt your head and the hips and shoulders will follow. Don't raise or straighten the head until you reach the straightaway. And never burn the turn!'

As Dina settled into the starting blocks she felt ready to spring out of them fast. She was getting better at conserving her energy before each race and using her nerves to propel her forward.

The gun fired.

Dina flew out of the blocks like a bullet. She eased into the bend effortlessly. As she approached the home straight, she told herself: 'That was a good turn, you can relax into the race from here.' She crossed the finish line to take first place in a personal best of 23.29 seconds, with Desirèe and Tessa finishing second and third respectively.

As the press clamoured to talk to her, Dina was still out of breath. At 17, she was the world's youngest medallist at a world athletics championships for 20 years. She had enough energy to smile and answer questions though.

After the ceremony, Dina and Desirèe hugged each other and clutched their gold and silver medals close to their chests. Yasmin and Steffi came running over to congratulate them.

'That was amazing!' they cried. 'You can't relax just yet, though!'

Dina and Desirèe looked at each other.

'No way! We've got a race to win tomorrow!'

Dina couldn't wait to run with the team the next day and had difficulty sleeping that night, as she ran over the events of the day in her head. She'd won a gold medal. Could she win another tomorrow?

It rained the following morning. The team sighed with relief that the air around the stadium had cooled as they walked out to the track. Dina took her place on the second leg; the longest stretch to run. She thought of Yasmin at the start, who she knew was nervous.

'I hope the baton won't be so wet from my sweat that I'll drop it!'

Dina reassured her. 'Don't worry, it'll all be over before you know it!'

They'd achieved a great time in the heats, but all of them wanted to break it.

A huge cheer from the crowd went up as the gun fired for the start of the race. Yasmin made good headway on the turn and sprinted towards Dina, who prepared to take the baton from her. After a seamless handover she pelted down the longest stretch towards Steffi, taking the lead and clearing at least two feet in the race. After she handed to

Steffi, she watched her pelt down the track towards Desirèe for the home straight. It was looking close. Déborah Sananes of France and Eefje Boons of the Netherlands were almost neck-and-neck with Desirèe.

'Come on Desirèe!' The team screamed at the top of their lungs as they watched her pound towards the finish line, determined to see off her challengers. When she crossed the line first, the three of them ran over to her laughing and crying, 'You did it! You did it!'

They leapt up and down as they checked their time on the board.

'43.81 seconds!' they all screamed in unison.

Not only had they won gold, but they'd also broken the UK junior record. Dina couldn't believe what an incredible year 2013 had been – and it wasn't over yet by any means.

CHAPTER 15

A HUGE OPPORTUNITY

Despite her successes in Italy, the athletics season wasn't over yet for Dina. As a result of her relay win, she was asked to run in the senior relay team at the 2013 London Anniversary Games.

Dina was thrilled not only return to the Olympic Stadium, but to help the team – consisting of Anyika Onuora, Annabelle Lewis and Ashleigh Nelson – take gold in 42.69 seconds, the fastest women's relay time in 12 years. This time she had been the first runner in the relay and it had caught the eye of the British selectors deciding the final line-up for the World Championships in Moscow the following month. One afternoon in the gym, Dina answered her phone. It was the coach Rana Reider.

'Oh, hi Rana,' said Dina nonchalantly.

'How would you like to come to Moscow with me?'

Dina couldn't believe her ears.

'What? Did you just say...?'

'Yes Dina, we'd like you to run in the 4 x 100 relay.'

Dina could hardly get her response out. At seventeen, she was still so young, yet they had faith in her.

'Are you kidding?'

Rana's reply was simple: 'Dina, we believe you can do this.'

'Thank you! Thank you for this opportunity!'

She knew this was a great opportunity to improve. She was no longer running against Europeans or juniors. She was competing against world champions.

However, she felt herself quivering a little when

she realised she'd be running against gold medallist and Olympic champion Shelly-Ann Fraser-Pryce in the relay. After her performances at London 2012, Shelly-Ann had been lauded as 'the greatest female sprinter of all time'.

John offered Dina some advice. 'Be inspired by her but don't be intimidated by her. Respect her but don't idolise her. Otherwise, you'll panic and lose concentration when you run.'

Dina nodded.

'You have just as much right to be there as they do,' added John. 'And this will help you to make the important transition from junior to senior.'

Dina laughed. 'I'll do my best to just think of her as a normal person.'

'She's not a superhero! Remember how nervous Mo Farah and Jess were? No doubt she'll be going through it too. Just concentrate on yourself.'

'Thanks, John.'

'And, remember, you're the youngest athlete to be selected for the Great Britain and Northern

Ireland Squad in these Championships.'

Dina smiled. As the least experienced in big championships, she'd been put on to start for the relay. She knew she'd benefit from her new team's combined extra years of track experience. Ashleigh Nelson, Annabelle Lewis and Hayley Jones all had personal bests that Dina knew would fare them well if they reached the final.

But as she took her starting place on lane three for the final, on a blazing hot afternoon at Luzhniki Stadium, her nerves kicked in. She stepped from side to side and tapped the baton nervously against her leg until she caught sight of her face on the screen, looking serious with her two side plaits tied back into a ponytail. She broke out into a smile, in an attempt to contradict how nervous she felt, and waved to the camera as a large cheer went up for her.

'Wow,' she said to herself. 'People are watching me run.' She'd never been in a position where she felt such a weight of responsibility. A feeling of horror went through her as she thought, 'The papers will hate me if I mess up! And I can't let my teammates down!' Their careers and aspirations were on the line too.

Great Britain's team had won the heat two hours earlier that afternoon in 42.75 seconds. But now they were running against the superb Jamaican and USA teams. Shelly-Ann Fraser-Pryce, for Jamaica, was standing on the very same track as Dina, waiting to take on the home stretch in the anchor leg. Dina had watched her take gold in the 100 and 200 metres in record times just a week before.

Just when Dina realised her negative thinking was beginning to spiral out of control, she remembered John's words: 'Respect her. Don't idolise her.'

She smiled as she thought of the Greek heroes she loved studying at school. She remembered the wreath she had drawn on her picture of Kelly Holmes' head. 'Come on Dina, focus, you can do this. Do a great start for your team.'

'On your marks...'

Dina felt the sweat seep through to the baton she was holding in her hand while the announcer said the words they were all waiting for. One last cheer went up from the crowd and then there was silence.

Dina took one last jump up and down before she settled into the blocks.

'Get set!'

Bang!

Dina flew out of the blocks and round the bend towards Ashleigh for the first handover. The change happened fast, and she watched with relief as Ashleigh tore off down the straight. But it was clearly Jamaica's race. Dina watched in awe as Shelly-Ann hared it down the last leg with a clear eight-metre lead, her pink strip of hair flying behind her. She looked for Hayley, who appeared to have been swallowed up by France and the USA, who took silver and bronze. Dina shook hands with the other competitors before she ran over to her teammates to celebrate.

'Great race, guys!'

Although they'd failed to make a place for Great Britain on the podium, they knew fourth place was not be sniffed at. They'd been up against some of the best teams in the world. And Dina was delighted to see Shelly-Ann run that fast in a record-winning race of 41.29 seconds, matching Usain Bolt's success and taking three medals at the Championships.

However, the team had news for her.

'We're going to contest it – we think France made an illegal changeover.'

They all watched Jamaica, France and the USA claim their medals, but after the ceremony their protest was upheld and the French team were disqualified. The girls jumped around for joy as they received confirmation of their bronze medal.

'I can't believe it!' Dina cried down the phone to her parents, who were watching the games back in England.

'You've done your country proud,' her mum replied.

She had. But Dina's bronze medal was also proof that she could compete on a world stage.

To cap an extraordinary 2013, just weeks before her eighteenth birthday, she was shortlisted for the BBC Young Sports Personality of the Year. She felt more ready than ever to make the move from junior to senior, and looked ahead with great anticipation to her first professional senior championships in Zurich the following year.

CHAPTER 16

WORLD JUNIOR CHAMPIONSHIPS

Dina and John stepped up her training at the beginning of 2014, with a view to qualifying for Zurich in August. Before that, she was also competing in the World Junior Championships in Eugene, Oregon.

'We'll focus on increasing your speed and performance, as always,' said John, 'and keep you in good shape – and if you do well in Eugene, you're a definite contender.'

He smiled, and added: 'It means you might have to spend less time in the nail bar, though.'

Dina laughed. 'No way, John, I'm putting my

foot down. It's become a tradition now.'

It was true. Before every important run, Dina visited the nail bar for an elaborate new design, from multi-coloured roses to hearts and geometric symbols. It was also a welcome distraction from studying hard for the final year of her A-levels.

The summer of 2014 would be a gruelling one for Dina, in terms of studying and training; at one point she had to manage a schedule for both her A-level Biology exam and her trials for the World Junior Championships in Oregon. She continued to run some great races throughout the season, racing the 200 metres at Bedford in 22.74 seconds and the 100 metres at Loughborough International in 11.20.

One afternoon, when Dina and John were looking over schedules, they realised Dina would find out her A-level results on the same day she would be running the heats for the 200 metres in Zurich.

John said: 'You'd better make sure you get what

you want then – we don't want that putting you off the race!'

Dina had her heart set on studying History at King's College in London and needed three A grades to get in.

It was hard to manage such a schedule of both training and studying, but that summer she received an endorsement that spurred her on even further.

One afternoon, she turned up to training to find a pile of Nike clothing waiting for her in the dressing room.

'What's all this?' she said to John. 'You been on a shopping spree?'

'It seems Nike would like to sponsor you.'

'What?'

'Good thing you already like their sportswear, eh?'

Dina beamed from ear to ear. They looked at each other. Although John was laidback about the news, the gravitas wasn't lost on either of them. She was now a professional getting paid to do what she loved.

'I guess it's not just my parents who believe in me now!'

She kept this at the forefront of her mind as she prepared for the 100 metres at the World Junior Championships in Eugene. She thought back on the last two years as she stared down the track. She'd won the heats the day before, she just needed to make sure her time didn't drop too much.

She said to herself: 'Dina, you've faced tougher races than this and succeeded. And you weren't running as fast as you are now back then. You can do this.'

'On your marks, get set...'

Bang!

She knew she'd made a great start as she sprang out of the blocks and raced down the straight, taking a comfortable lead against Ecuador's Ángela Tenorio and the USA's Kaylin Whitney. When she crossed the finish line, she threw her hands up in the air as she heard the crowd cheer. Her time was 11.23 seconds! The words flashed up on the screen:

'Dina Asher-Smith: World Junior Champion!' She struggled to hold back her emotions, as she hugged and congratulated the other athletes on their run, including Desirèe who'd come in fourth.

As the sun dipped in the stadium, Dina wrapped herself in the British flag and chatted excitedly to reporters.

'What are your hopes and dreams for the future?' they asked.

'I can't even think right now – I'm just over the moon to have won!'

Her first senior competition in Zurich was less than a month away. Could she repeat her triumph in her first senior competition?

CHAPTER 17

A NERVOUS WAIT

Dina watched the sun sparkle on the clear blue waters of Lake Zurich as the coach rounded the streets towards Letzigrund Stadium. It was a beautiful day and, as much as she tried to distract herself with the sights of the city, her stomach was churning. It was the morning of her A-level results and she wished she could be back in London with her parents. She kept desperately trying to log on to her school's system to collect them but couldn't get any internet connection on her phone. She wanted to know those results before she started warming up for the 200 metres heats that day.

On the coach her fellow British athletes Jodie Williams and Bianca Williams tried to reassure her.

'You'll smash those A-levels, Dina!' said Bianca.

'And the heats!' Jodie agreed. 'We're both shaking with nerves at the thought of facing you in the final!'

At 20 years old, Bianca and Jodie were both a couple of years older than Dina and were more experienced athletes who'd won at the Commonwealth Championships. Dina felt very proud to have the opportunity to run against them. She'd seen Jodie pull a hamstring back in 2012 at the Olympic trials so she was pleased to see her back in shape now.

'Thanks, guys,' she said with a smile.

The coach neared the stadium. 'Ah well,' thought Dina, 'I'll just have to be patient and put it out of my mind.'

Suddenly, her phone beeped. It was a message from her mum. She had to double blink a few times to check she'd read it correctly: 'Three A's! Well done! Huge love, mum xx.'

'OMG!' Dina shouted out before texting back frantically: 'Are you sure?'

'Yes, I've just logged onto your account,' came the reply.

Jodie and Bianca patted her on the back. 'Good news then?'

Relief washed over Dina. 'I can't believe it! I'm going to King's! This is the best morning of my life!'

It was about to get even better. Later that morning she won the first round of heats in the 200 metres in 22.65 seconds.

But despite her great performance, Dina would still be denied her place in the final the next day. Just beforehand, while she warmed up in lane six, she took a final look down at her purple and yellow Nike trainers and felt a twinge in her hamstring. She put it out of her mind as a roar from the crowd went up for her, the youngest athlete in the race. But, when she propelled out of the blocks and approached the first bend, she felt the pain grow sharper.

'Ouch!' she cried out. She remembered John's warning about pushing her body too far. She slowed down and pulled over to the side, and watched Jodie win silver and the Netherlands' Dafne Schippers take gold.

Dina's summer of athletics may have been over, but at least she had a new academic year to look forward to at King's.

***

Dina's mum put her head round the door of her daughter's bedroom.

'Is that Duke I can hear?'

Dina looked up and nodded. She was busy revising for end-of-term exams.

'Bit different to the tempo I normally hear coming out of your bedroom.'

Dina laughed.

'I find some jazz a lot more relaxing for studying. I'll keep Jay-Z for warm-ups though! I've been thinking, I might do my dissertation on Duke Ellington.'

'You're studying History, aren't you?'

'It's all related. That's what I love so much about history.'

Her mum looked at her proudly and said: 'I think you're going to make your own history.'

'Whatever, Mum. You would say that!'

But her mum's prediction was about to come true – sooner than she thought.

In March 2015, Dina competed in the European Indoor Championships in Prague. As she flew over the city with John, she still had to pinch herself that athletics gave her the opportunity to visit such beautiful cities.

At the beginning of that year, her 60-metre time was hovering around 7.33. She'd worked on getting it down to 7.14 throughout February but wanted to improve on her personal best further.

'I want to get to 7.10, John.'

He told her: 'Go for 7.08 and you'll match Jeanette Kwakye's record.'

Jeanette was a three-time British champion who'd retired in 2014, and Dina made it her goal to equal her time.

In the heats she performed brilliantly and came in first at 7.10 seconds. She knew the final would be tougher, though; she would face Dafne Schippers, the fastest European woman.

John reminded her: 'Just concentrate on reaching your best.'

In the final, Dina spotted that Dafne was wearing her favourite purple and yellow Nike trainers. While Dina was in lane seven, Dafne was to her right in lane eight.

'I'm pleased I picked my pink ones,' Dina thought to herself. She took a final glance at her nails before she settled into the blocks. She'd decided on gold for this race, a bold statement for what she aimed to win.

'On your marks... get set...'

Bang!

Dina made a good start. With 20 metres to go she was leading, but it wasn't long before she felt the strength of the champion Dafne overtaking her to take gold. But as Dina crossed the finish line to take silver, she knew – even before checking the board – that she'd run a great time.

She hugged Dafne, who had run a record speed of 7.05 seconds, and then saw her own time flash up. It was 7.08. She had beaten her time and matched Kwakye's record. She ran over to the side to celebrate with John.

'I did it, John!'

Uncharacteristically for John, he was smiling away. 'Well done, Dina. Not only have you matched a British record, you're now the fastest teenager ever at 60 metres!'

Dina shook her head in disbelief. But, despite the record-breakers, she knew she couldn't relax yet. She had a full summer of athletics championships ahead of her: from the FBK Games in the Netherlands to the London Anniversary Games and the World Athletics Championships in Beijing. There were always more records to beat and champions to take on.

CHAPTER 18

HENGELO, LONDON, BEIJING, RIO

At the Fanny Blankers-Koen Games in the Dutch city of Hengelo, Dina was warming up in lane six, and chuckled to find herself next to Dafne Schippers once again. Not that this put her off: she looked down the track, feeling confident she was going to run a great 100 metres, and, if anything, she was thankful for runners like Dafne who spurred her on to be better.

She knew that Dafne was working towards running the race in under 11 seconds, which would set a new national record for her country. But Dina had her own goals. She'd worked solidly on the race with John and had reduced her time to 11.15 two weeks before in Manchester. Today, she wanted to break the British world record.

'On your marks, get set...'

Bang!

Dina blasted out of the blocks. It was an excellent start and for the first half of the race she was almost neck-and-neck with Dafne. But in the last 10 metres the Dutch champion took a clear lead and flew over the finishing line in a record breaking 10.94 seconds. Still, Dina had her own reason to celebrate too. She jumped for joy as her score flashed up on the board: 11.02 seconds. She'd smashed her own personal best but also broken the British world record for the 100 metres, beating the previous time of 11.05, held by Montell Douglas.

Dina arrived home to a hero's welcome at Blackheath and Bromley. They'd made her carrot cake: her favourite. The coaches and athletes gathered around, and they asked her what record she wanted to beat next.

Dina already knew. She had her heart set on running the 100 metres in under 11 seconds. If Dafne could do it, so could she.

***

Two months later, in July 2015, Dina took her chance at the London Anniversary Games. As she took in the clear blue skies surrounding the Olympic Park, she remembered three years earlier, when she stood at the side of the track as a box carrier, watching the athletes who would become the heroes of Super Saturday. She had hoped the races would attract crowds but never dreamt the stands would fill to their 40,000 capacity. She felt excited, rather than nervous. Although she wanted to achieve her next record, ultimately, she just loved to race. It was her first heat and she breathed a sigh of relief she wasn't racing against Dafne, although she knew Murielle Ahouré, to her left, was a strong contender with a speed of 10.81 seconds.

'On your marks, get set...'

Bang!

As Dina left the blocks, she told herself off. She'd not made a great start and Murielle led. But she lifted her knees high and pumped down the straight stretch to overtake and keep her at bay. When she crossed the line first she knew she'd run a good race. A roar went up from the crowd and she knew before she even looked at the board that she'd hit her record. There it was – yellow figures in stark contrast against the black background: 10.99 seconds. She put her thumbs up to the crowd and waved. She was the first British woman in history to run 100 metres in under 11 seconds.

As she joined her parents at the side, her mother could barely speak.

'I always feel kind of helpless when you run... but you amaze me every time!'

It was a fantastic achievement and Dina wanted to match or beat her new time in the final. But it wasn't to be. Dafne took gold, running an incredible time of 10.92, while Dina finished fourth with a time of 11.06 seconds. At the end of the race, they hugged each other.

Dina laughed. 'One day I'll catch up with you!'

'I think you will too. See you in Beijing, Dina!'

Their summer wasn't over yet. They were both competing in the World Championships in China that August.

***

In Beijing, Dina did not manage to qualify for the 100 metres final, but nevertheless watched in awe when Shelly-Ann Fraser-Pryce and Dafne Schippers took gold and silver respectively. She was also disappointed not to have the chance to visit any of the city's top tourist spots, but at least she had qualified for the final of the 200 metres, and the crowd at the Beijing National Stadium cheered as she and her fellow competitors prepared themselves for the race.

Dina had run two personal bests in the last two heats, even beating Dafne's times. However, as with every race, she knew it came down to her performance on the day. 'As long as I achieve another personal best,' thought Dina.

The gun fired and Dina took off down the track. She started well, but it was clear the race belonged to Dafne and the two Jamaicans, Elaine Thompson and Veronica Campbell Brown, who charged ahead to cross the finish line first. Dina came in at fifth place but she leapt up and down when she saw her time: 22.07!

Even though she hadn't won a medal, the spectators and press knew for sure now that the British athlete was incredibly special and had the potential to be a future world champion.

At 19 years old, she'd become the fastest teenager in history, a title previously owned by her hero, Olympic champion Allyson Felix. Her time of 22.07 seconds in the 200 metres also broke a British record set by Kathy Cook in 1984, 11 years before

Dina was born.

Dina's eyes shone as she spoke excitedly to the press: 'To run against such incredible elite athletes was an honour in itself. I've hit three PBs, three days running and am so happy to have ended with a record.'

***

A year later, Dina had to pinch herself to make sure she wasn't dreaming about competing in the 2016 Rio Olympics. She glanced up towards Corcovado, the mountain that overlooked the Olympic Stadium. Brazil had always appealed to her as an exciting and vibrant place with a fascinating history, with its melting pot of African and European cultures that had helped to create the offbeat syncopated rhythms of bossa nova.

Dina had come fifth in the 200 metres in an admirable time of 22.31. But it wasn't enough to beat athletes on the international stage. However, she had one last chance to win a medal in the relay team.

She was back with her old friend Desirèe Henry for the relay, along with new teammates Daryll Neita and Asha Philip. They'd spent the summer practising their performance on the new site at Loughborough and had built a great team dynamic. Asha, the eldest at 25, kept them in check when they lost their focus or when the impulsive nature of Daryll, the youngest, took hold. And their belief in their team grew stronger as they demonstrated their skill and strength at the European Championships, taking away silver, losing out to a strong Dutch team.

'On your marks, get set...'

Bang!

Dina watched as Tianna Bartoletta of the USA and Christania Williams of Jamaica shot off on the first leg. They'd both made the incredible starts everyone expected, but so had Asha and she wasn't far behind them before the first handover to Desirèe. Desirèe took the baton and covered considerable ground to take fourth place behind Jamaica, the USA and Germany, passing to Dina, who increased their lead on the third leg. After a seamless handover to Daryll, Dina cheered as she watched her ward off challenges on the home straight from Germany's Rebekka Haase to take third place behind the USA in first and Jamaica in second.

The British team leapt around for joy as the enormity of their win against the two athletic powerhouses sank in.

'Bronze! We've won a medal!'

They'd also broken the British record that night, with a new time of 41.77 seconds. As Dina stood on the podium with the rest of her team to claim bronze, she felt as though – from that moment on – anything was possible.

CHAPTER 19

A
SETBACK

It was the start of 2017 and Dina was performing plyometric jumps in one of her final training sessions before competing in the Birmingham Indoor Grand Prix. On the last jump, she misjudged the ledge of the bench and fell back on to the floor. She cried out in pain as she tried to get back up again. John rushed over and instructed her not to move. Dina winced as her physio, Martin Wilson, came over to take a closer look.

'No!' Dina cried out in frustration when she was told she had fractured her foot. She turned to John.

'Well, you definitely can't do Birmingham on Saturday.'

Dina's mind raced ahead to the World Athletics Championships that August. The games were being hosted in the Olympic Stadium in London and Dina was desperate to take part.

She was told her foot would take at least eight weeks to heal, and that it might not be possible to get back in shape in time for August.

Dina groaned. 'I can't believe it John – how stupid!'

'I know, don't kick yourself for it, though.'

Dina couldn't help but smile at his terrible joke, although the timing seemed incredibly unfair and inconvenient. But she wasn't going to let this jeopardise her career. Later that day she tweeted: 'So upset and frustrated but it was a freak accident, one of those unavoidable things in life, I guess. Comeback starts now.'

Dina held on to her dream to be part of the World Athletics Championships. There was no way she was going to miss that, not after experiencing the thrill of 2012 in the Olympic Stadium.

A few days before her operation she went to meet John and the Olympic relay team at a training session. As she arrived on crutches, the other girls in the relay team ran over to greet her.

'Oh Dina, it's so good to see you! But shouldn't you be resting?'

Dina looked at them defiantly. 'Guys, I'm going to make the team. We're a great relay team, do you think I'd let you down?! I want us to get silver this time – it's too important!'

They all avoided her eye contact as she continued to beam confidently at them. John also looked away.

'Just wait and see! I'm going to be able to run in August. So I might as well come to all the meetings. I don't want to miss out on team bonding.'

Desirèe looked at her with surprise. 'Dina, I can't believe how upbeat you are!'

Daryll shook her head. 'You're an inspiration.'

She shrugged. 'Oh guys, whatever.'

Dina put the doubtful faces of John, Martin and the relay team out of her mind as she underwent surgery on her foot to insert two screws. She'd heard stories of athletes who weren't able to run for two years after fractures, but she was determined that wouldn't be her.

Even so, it wasn't easy. The day after her plaster was removed, she gasped as she tried to put the kettle on to make a cup of tea. She couldn't even get on her tiptoes. She cried out in frustration. If simple tasks were this challenging, how would she rebuild the strength in her muscles for the Championships? She'd expected some muscle loss but was downhearted to discover just how much. It was April and she only had four months to be fighting fit for the Championships. It would be another three months until she could train properly too.

To add to her pressures, she was in her last year of university and needed to finish her dissertation. She vowed that she wouldn't waste a single hour of her time. In between poring over her academic notes and writing her dissertation at her laptop, she continued to focus on building up her muscle strength with John and Martin. As well as supervising her gentle exercises on an underwater treadmill, they worked on her balance and coordination too. By the first of July, Dina was preparing to run in the 100 metres in the British Athletics Championships in Birmingham. Her muscles weren't yet back to their full strength, but she felt strong enough to compete.

John looked at her in astonishment as she jumped up and down excitedly.

'It feels so great to be on spikes again!' she said.

And she had another reason to celebrate.

'I've finally got my dissertation in – yippee!'

'Please, Dina, save your excitement for the track.' John was hesitant to share in the celebrations, but he, like everyone else, was impressed with her positive mental attitude.

That day she came sixth in the 100 metres, achieving a time of 11.53 seconds. It was a slower time than any of her personal bests the year before. But it felt great to race again and she knew she was on the road to recovery and would continue to improve.

But there was one question hanging over her. Would she be fast enough to compete in the 200 metres or relay race at the World Championships in the Olympic Stadium? With just six weeks to go, there was little time to train for the event.

CHAPTER 20

WORLD CHAMPIONSHIPS: OLYMPIC PARK 2017

The roar from the crowd reverberated in Dina's ears as she shot out of the blocks and started to round the bend on the 200-metre track for the IAFF (now World Athletics) Championships at the Olympic Park. Their cheers of support, love and encouragement were all that she needed to power her down the home straight. Any doubts or fears she'd been feeling before the race melted away, and she soared towards the finishing line to take fourth place.

She looked up at the clock and grinned from ear to ear. She hadn't taken a medal, but she didn't care. She'd achieved a new personal best of 22.22 seconds, in front of one of the most supportive home crowds she'd ever experienced.

Dina hugged and congratulated the other competitors, and felt relieved that she'd trusted her own instincts and not listened to the doubts of people around her. She was on the road to recovery and felt ready to put the injury behind her. John shook his head in disbelief at Dina's flushed and happy face.

'I wouldn't have believed it was possible, Dina,' he said, 'after only six weeks of training.'

'John, that was amazing! I felt like the crowd was literally pushing me to the finish line!'

'They were right behind you, Dina.'

'Never doubt me again, eh, John?'

'I never did.'

'It might sound a little crazy, but I think this has done me good in the long term.'

John raised his eyebrows.

'Seriously, look,' she went on, 'a medal would have been fantastic of course. But I know what I'm capable of overcoming now. I'll face any other setbacks with more confidence.'

John smiled and, with a twinkle in his eye, said: 'Great! How about I break the other foot then?!'

Dina cried out in protest. 'John, that's not funny!'

A few days later, Dina was gearing up to perform in front of another packed London stadium. This time the crowd were cheering on Dina, Asha, Daryl and Desirèe as they prepared to run the 4 x 100 metres relay. They needed all the support they could get as they were about to take on the reigning champions: the USA and Jamaica.

Yet again, relief washed over Dina.

'I wouldn't have missed this for anything,' she thought as she made her way to the third leg on lane five and placed her marker on the track for the baton handover.

Relays were as problematic as any other race and the team knew they could never quite predict the outcome. They were facing a strong USA team that consisted of Allyson Felix and Tori Bowie. But when Dina looked down at her pink and yellow Nikes she felt confident. She had also applied eyeliner and eye shadow before the race, to help her relax. As she always said: 'If we win a medal, I want to be looking my best!'

Desirèe laughed. 'Won't it be smeared all over your face by then?'

'Extra waterproof, of course! In case I start crying!'

'On your marks... get set...'

Bang!

The USA and Jamaica proved to be tough competition and took the lead comfortably, just as the British team had expected. While Desirèe was pelting down the track on the second leg, Dina began to run in preparation for the handover. When she took the baton, Jamaica's Simone Facey and the USA's Morolake Akinosun had a clear 10-metre lead on her.

'I can make a difference here,' thought Dina as she fought her way down the third leg, hot on their heels. After she handed the baton to Daryll for the home stretch, she cheered her on. Daryll charged ahead of Jamaica's Sashalee Forbes to lead the team to a silver medal in a record time of 42.12 seconds.

Journalists gathered to interview a British team who understood the significance of what they'd achieved. To take a step up from bronze in Rio was fantastic enough but to do it on home turf meant the world to them. The team were so proud to win the medal in London.

But the celebrations weren't over for Dina that summer. The following week, she graduated from university with a 2:1.

'No more essays!' She danced around her room, thinking of the 61 essays she'd completed over the past three years. However, she wasn't sure she wanted to give up academia completely and began to consider studying law.

Her mum looked at her in astonishment.

'Dina, how about you give yourself a break for a little while?'

Dina joked: 'You know what would happen if I took too long a break, Mum, I'd just end up eating pizzas my whole life!'

But she knew her mum had a point. She was pleased to put the stress of studying behind her and focus on being a full-time professional athlete. For the next few months, she focused on training for her first ever Commonwealth Games in Australia.

The Games weren't until April 2018, but Dina flew out a month early to the preparation camp in Brisbane, an hour away from the Gold Coast venue. She wanted to get accustomed to training and competing in 28-degree heat. In a year without the Olympics or World Championships to compete in, she wanted to focus on the 200 metres at the Games and run against the fastest in the world. And, of course, it was great to train in warm temperatures in the early months of the year on the beach.

This time she was representing England, rather

than Team GB, and so, instead of a Union Jack, her kit was emblazoned with a single red lion.

A huge cheer went up from the crowd as the announcer read out the competitors in the 200 metres final: 'In lane six, Dina Asher-Smith!' It always made a difference to hear that support. Dina listened for the sound of her mum cheering, which always spurred her on in each race: 'Go on, Dina!' She was overjoyed her parents had flown across the world to see her compete and that her friends back home were organising sleepovers to ensure they stayed up and didn't miss her race.

To her right in lane seven was Jamaica's Olympic double gold medallist, Elaine Thompson, one of the fastest women in the world.

Dina told herself: 'This is why you chose to be here. To run and compete against the best. But forget all that right now. Just spring out of the blocks – and run!'

'On your marks... get set...'

Bang!

Dina flew out of the blocks and took a clear lead. But on the last 20 metres there was a challenge to her left as the Bahamian athlete Shaunae Miller-Uibo and Jamaican Shericka Jackson overtook her to take gold and silver respectively. But Dina had come in at 22.29 seconds to take bronze, just ahead of Elaine Thompson who'd taken fourth place, and so was ecstatic with her result.

But it wasn't the only medal Dina took away from the Games. Two days later she helped the women's Team England relay team take gold in a new British record of 42.46 seconds that defeated the defending Jamaicans.

She told John her goals for the coming year. 'I'm going to get my 200 metres in under 22 seconds. And I know I've got a 10.80 in me for the 100 metres.'

As she flew over Australia clutching her two medals, she thought ahead to the European Championships in Berlin that summer. She knew she had to work hard to keep her promise to John.

CHAPTER 21

EUROPEAN CHAMPIONSHIPS: BERLIN

In the call-up room, waiting to go out on to the track at Berlin's Olympiastadion, Dina could feel her nerves rising. She was about to run the final of the 100 metres. But even her usual distraction tricks of focusing on 'normal' things like hair and make-up weren't working. She'd been working hard all year to this point and she was happy with how she'd performed in the semi-final earlier that day, coming first with 10.93 seconds. She'd broken a record in Oslo in June of 10.92, beating her previous record of 10.99. But still, she felt uneasy.

Would she stumble? Would there be a headwind? There were fears she couldn't quite shake, for some reason.

John knew better than to distract Dina from her pre-race rituals, but he could see something was on her mind and that these were no ordinary race nerves.

'What's up, Dina?'

She sighed. 'I dunno.'

'Are you thinking about the start in your semi-final earlier?'

Dina nodded, with some relief. It was rare she could ever hide what she was thinking from John.

'It wasn't a bad start,' John said.

'No, it wasn't.'

'You know what, Dina, just do your normal start.'

'Normal?'

'Yes, normal.'

As she settled into the starting blocks, she realised they were the only words she had needed to hear. Two lanes to her left was Dafne Schippers, who she'd still never beaten.

'Normal start, Dina, normal start,' she repeated to herself.

'On your marks... get set...'

Bang!

She tore out of the blocks and took the lead from the start, a clear half-metre ahead of her competitors. She crossed the line first and leapt for joy as her time flashed up: 10.85 seconds!

'Yes!'

Dafne was one of the first to congratulate her. 'You got me, Dina!'

'I said I would one day!'

The next day Dina won gold in the 200 metres in 21.89 seconds, beating Dafne into second place.

It was a new record. Dina was now the fastest British woman in history and the first to run below 22 seconds for 200 metres.

But she continued to fly that week. In the 4 x 100 relay race, she was picked for the anchor leg, tearing down the home straight to beat off a challenge from the Dutch sprinter, Naomi Sedney, and take gold for Britain.

Dina took away three gold medals from Berlin. All eyes were on this star athlete, who was already demonstrating great Olympic potential for Tokyo.

John kept her grounded though. 'She's done okay,' he responded gruffly as the media clamoured to speak to her.

Dina shook her head. 'One day John, I'll make you cry.'

'Make that your next goal!'

'I will, John.'

Later that year, Dina was named Women's European Athlete of the Year and was hailed by Sebastian Coe as the next sprint sensation in athletics to follow in Jessica Ennis's footsteps. Not only had she become hugely successful during 2018, but also rather famous.

CHAPTER 22

WORLD CHAMPIONSHIPS: DOHA

Dina continued to train for the rest of 2018, but her success in Berlin and her newfound fame brought with it many exciting new opportunities. Towards the end of the year she was included on Forbes' 30 Under 30 lists, and asked to model for Paris Fashion Week.

John rolled his eyes and quipped: 'Well, this is all we need, you already spend enough time on make-up before a race!'

'The track is my red carpet, thanks John!

'Well, please, no shimmying down the track – we won't improve your times that way!'

Dina fell about laughing but was genuinely happy to be asked. She loved fashion and particularly enjoyed supporting British fashion designers. But in early 2019 she received the ultimate accolade when Stormzy asked her to be part of a collective of young and inspirational black Britons for a cover he was curating for the magazine *Elle*. Although she continued to shrug off suggestions that she was a role model, she was beginning to realise she had a voice to champion the causes she cared about. She began contributing to a women's sports column to celebrate women's achievements in sport and help tackle their under-representation in the media.

Despite her newfound fame, Dina knew she had to keep setting goals with John, in order to stay grounded and to avoid becoming complacent.

One morning, John called her up, just a week after she'd come back from a sport-launching event organised by Nike in Paris. She was still reeling from the fact that she'd met Naomi Campbell.

'Right, I know you've been swanning about with

celebs but if you're not down at Norman Park within the hour, I'm coming round there to drag you out.'

'John, I've just ordered a Domino's!'

'What? You do want to get below 10.85 seconds this year, don't you?'

'Okay, John, okay!' She groaned but was grateful for his grounding influence. No matter where she might go or whoever she might meet, she still had their training schedule to stick to for the new year: four hours a day, six days a week. She smiled to herself as she realised she couldn't ever see herself being coached by anyone else but John. The fact she'd stuck with him since she was nine said as much.

Throughout the summer of 2019, Dina ran some formidable times at the British Championships and Anniversary Games, but she hadn't yet matched her time of 10.85 for the 100 metres. She knew she would have to break her own record to beat Shelly-Ann Fraser-Pryce, who she lost out to on silver. And she was yet to run the 200 metres in under 22 seconds, a time that John was certain she could achieve.

However, the year still wasn't over. Expectations were running high for the World Championships in Doha that autumn and Dina put anything that might distract her or pile on the pressure to one side, which included a ban on social media four weeks up to the event. Bets were already on that she could be the first Briton to become a 200 metres gold champion, a feat not yet achieved.

***

As a gentle breeze blew around the Khalifa International Stadium in Doha, she knew she had to put the expectations of the crowd to one side. Dina thanked her lucky stars again that the 100 metres final was at night to avoid the intense temperatures of the day. She'd already felt her energy flag a little after the last two days of heats. But now, she had to run, run, run as fast as she could possibly could.

No matter that the world champion and sprinting legend Shelly-Ann was right next to her in lane six, with her multi-coloured hair sway from side to side in a ponytail. Shelly-Ann Fraser-Pryce – her hero, and now her equal.

Dina still had to pinch herself. She was running against such world-class athletes. 'Don't think about that now,' Dina told herself. 'The next 10 seconds are all that counts.'

'On your marks... get set...'

Bang!

As she took off down the track, she ran with all the passion and desire to win that she'd always had. But it wasn't to be, and she was beaten into second place and a silver medal by Shelly-Ann by 0.12 seconds.

But, at 10.83 seconds, Dina had still beaten her personal best and had set a new national British record. She was also the first British woman in 36 years to win a World Championships sprint medal.

During the medal ceremony, Dina was shocked

when Shelly-Ann looked down from the top podium and said to her: 'You're an inspiration. You'll be at the top soon. I'm sure of it.'

Dina felt the tears well up in her eyes as the enormity of those words began to sink in. With just one year to go until the Tokyo Olympics, she was moving closer to her dream.

But she still couldn't afford to get distracted. She had heats for the 200 metres the next day to focus on. Could she finally run it under 22 seconds? And win gold for her country?

Three nights later, Dina looked out on to the track of Khalifa International Stadium.

'This is it,' she said to herself. 'This is your race.'

She'd come top of the heats over the past two days, running 22.32 and 22.16 seconds, respectively. She was tired but knew she had reserved just enough energy for this last push, to run under 22 seconds for the final. Dina turned back to John and gave him a huge smile.

She could tell he was nervous. More than he

normally was. She knew how much this race meant to him, as well as her. But, as ever, he remained calm, repeating the words that had become customary before each race.

'Don't hold the horses, Dina.'

She nodded at him and smiled.

Yes, John believed in her but ultimately it was always down to her to deliver. And they both knew anything could happen in a race: a false start, a sudden headwind, a sudden burst of speed from a competitor. But as she walked on to the track and waved to the crowds, she felt an almost overwhelming sense of excitement build up inside her. She couldn't wait to unleash her excited energy on the track.

'On your marks...'

The crowd fell silent.

'Get set...'

Dina took one last look at her nails she'd painted a pale pink for the event.

She told herself: 'Just run – as fast as you can.' It

was the only thing she needed to tell herself in that moment.

Bang!

Dina flew out of the blocks. Above the roar of the crowd she tuned in for the cries of her mother that always helped to keep her centred in the race, while everything else passed by in such a flash.

Dina blazed around the turn, warding off challenges from the USA's Brittany Brown and Anglerne Annelus. As she went into the home straight she knew she had it. The race was hers. She crossed the line in 21.88 to take gold. She clasped her hands to her face as everyone ran to congratulate her. By running the race in under 22 seconds, she'd not only beaten her own personal best but made history for her country. Dina was now the first British female athlete to ever win a global sprint title.

She managed to contain her emotions until she saw the sight of her mum bounding down the steps of the stadium, with her dad following close behind, as always. Then the tears of relief and joy flowed. As she hugged them for what felt like an eternity, she felt a tap on her shoulder.

She turned to see John standing behind her and saw that his eyes were looking mistier than normal.

'Ha! Is that a tear in your eye, John?'

'You've done it. You've run the race I always knew you could run.'

Three days later, Dina brought home another medal for Britain, winning silver with Asha, Ashleigh and Daryll in the 4 x 100 relay, in 41.85 seconds. She returned home, a world champion and hero.

CHAPTER 23

THE FUTURE IS BRIGHT

'It's funny, you may be a world champion but you look exactly the same!'

Mrs Carty stretched out her arms to greet Dina at the reception of Perry Hall Primary School.

Dina laughed. 'Hopefully I've grown a bit!'

'It's the smile, I think. It just hasn't changed.'

'Well, it has changed here,' said Dina as she walked the corridors of her old school.

'Wait till you see the track and field facilities, they've changed quite a bit.'

Dina was introduced to another teacher, whose face she recognised.

'My name's Louise,' said the teacher. 'I was the

year above you here.'

Dina replied, 'Oh yes! I remember you.'

'I look after the running club now. It's become so popular! All the kids want to do is join now they know you went here; you're a hero to them!'

Dina blushed. 'That's so great more kids want to get into athletics.'

She thought of the speech Darren had given at her secondary school. 'Whether or not they want to turn professional, there's nothing quite like just running in a straight line, the wind in your hair.'

She looked out of the window towards the field where she'd first raced Mrs Carty. How long ago it all was.

'Well, you've made it all look possible, you see.'

They made their way towards Dina's old classroom.

'They're very excited about seeing you,' said Louise.

'That's an understatement,' said Mrs Carty.

Dina heard the hushed whispers of: 'She's here!

She's here!'

Louise opened the door, and Dina saw a sea of excited faces staring up at her. Gosh, she thought, this is more nerve-wracking than running!

'Hello everybody!'

'Now, we're very lucky to have Dina with us today,' said Mrs Carty. 'As you know, she used to go to school here.'

Dina nodded. 'Yes, this place is very important to me as it's where I first started running.'

'Now, who's got a question for Dina?'

A slew of hands went up.

'Wow!' said Dina, who suddenly felt very overwhelmed.

'Please! Can we see your medals, Miss?'

'Yes, of course!'

The children all scrambled to take a close look as she took them off from around her neck.

One girl pointed at the gold medal she'd won in Doha. 'Is that from the Olympics, Miss?'

'Ah no, I've not won a medal for an individual

race in the Olympics. Well, not yet, that is!'

Another voice piped up: 'Are you going to win in Tokyo, Miss?'

Dina smiled. 'Funny, you're not the only one who's been asking me that, you know.'

Then she thought for a moment, and added, 'I will do all I can to win at Tokyo, yes.'

'Can you come back when you win the Olympics?'

Dina burst out laughing. 'I certainly will. And I'll make sure I'm wearing a laurel wreath on my head too.'

Turn the page for a sneak preview
of another brilliant story in
the Ultimate Sports Heroes series. . .

TOM DALEY

Available now!

CHAPTER 1

BUDAPEST BRILLIANCE

22 July 2017

Tom Daley could barely breathe as he watched his rival, Chen Aisen, poised on the edge of the platform. It was the final of the men's 10-metre platform event at the World Aquatic Championships in Budapest and the tension around the pool was electric. Tom led Chen by a margin of just 5.7 points, but both divers had one more dive to perform. With so little difference between their scores, anything could happen. Tom swallowed nervously. He could see the determination and focus in his rival's eyes. If the Chinese diver – the Olympic champion – delivered a spectacular dive, the gold medal could easily slip from Tom's grasp.

The crowd hushed. Chen leapt from the board and into the air, turning a series of elegant somersaults before dropping neatly into the pool. Cheers rang around the auditorium. Tom gulped. It was a spectacular dive. His eyes flicked to the scoreboard: 106.20. A huge score! It would be very hard to beat.

Chen clambered from the pool, grinning. His teammates clustered around him, buzzing with noisy congratulations. Chen didn't even glance at Tom, standing on the top platform. *He thinks he's won,* Tom realised. *They don't think I can beat him. Well. We'll see about that.*

Tom's competitive spark had been lit. Adrenaline surged through him. He knew he would need the dive of his life to beat Chen. But he had nothing to lose. He would give his all in this final dive.

Here goes.

For a fraction of a second, it felt to Tom as though he was flying, soaring above the pool with his arms stretched out like wings. As gravity started to tug him downwards, he gripped his knees to his chest and tipped into his first somersault. Round and round he spun, suspended in mid-air, faster, faster. As he tumbled out of his final somersault, the only direction was down, down, down, plummeting at top speed towards the shimmering blue pool below.

As Tom hit the water, an explosion of cheers rocked the auditorium. Up in the stands, Tom's mum, Debbie, let out a cry of delight. Tom's husband, Lance, flung his arms into the air, while at the side of the pool, Tom's coach, Jane, jumped up and down for joy and his Great Britain teammates shrieked and whooped.

Tom could hear the cacophony of sound as he kicked back to the surface.

Was it good? It must have been good for the crowd to be cheering like this!

With eyes on the scoreboard, he blinked in disbelief: 106.20 points. The same score as Chen! It was enough to keep him on top. He had done it. He had beaten the Olympic champion.

Tom ran straight to Jane and gave her a joyful hug. She had supported and believed in him every step of the way. His teammates crowded round, bombarding him with hugs and kisses.

Meanwhile, his amazing mum and his wonderful husband, his most loyal supporters, were hurrying down from the stands, waiting to fling their arms around the new world champion. Tom felt like he was being swept up in a tidal wave of love, pride and support. He couldn't take the smile off his face. The victory was his. But it also belonged to his family, his friends, his teammates, his coach, his physiotherapist, his fans... everyone who had come on this incredible journey with him.

And at just 23, Tom knew he had much, much more to give. This journey wasn't over yet!

DINA ASHER-SMITH HONOURS

Olympic Medals

🏆 Rio 2016: 4 x 100 m Relay, Bronze

World Championship Medals

🏆 Moscow 2013: 4 x 100 m Relay, Bronze

🏆 London 2017: 4 x 100 m Relay, Silver

🏆 Doha 2019: 100 m, Silver;

4 x 100 m Relay, Silver;

200 m, Gold

NAME:	Dina Asher-Smith
DATE OF BIRTH:	**4 December 1995**
PLACE OF BIRTH:	Orpington, UK
NATIONALITY:	**British**
SPORT:	Athletics
Height:	**164 cm**
Main events:	100 m, 200 m & 4 x 100 m Relay
Club:	**Blackheath & Bromley**
Coach:	John Blackie

Olympic Medals

GOLD 0 SILVER  0 BRONZE 1

World Championship Medals

GOLD 1 SILVER 3 BRONZE 1